CW01239347

The Wonderful Adventures of Nils

You are holding a reproduction of an original work that is in the public domain in the United States of America, and possibly other countries. You may freely copy and distribute this work as no entity (individual or corporate) has a copyright on the body of the work. This book may contain prior copyright references, and library stamps (as most of these works were scanned from library copies). These have been scanned and retained as part of the historical artifact.

This book may have occasional imperfections such as missing or blurred pages, poor pictures, errant marks, etc. that were either part of the original artifact, or were introduced by the scanning process. We believe this work is culturally important, and despite the imperfections, have elected to bring it back into print as part of our continuing commitment to the preservation of printed works worldwide. We appreciate your understanding of the imperfections in the preservation process, and hope you enjoy this valuable book.

THE WONDERFUL ADVENTURES OF NILS

By Selma Lagerlof

✤ ✤

JERUSALEM, A Novel
(Trans from Swedish by Velma Swanston Howard)
CHRIST LEGENDS
(Trans from Swedish by Velma Swanston Howard)
WONDERFUL ADVENTURES OF NILS
(Trans. from Swedish by Velma Swanston Howard)
FURTHER ADVENTURES OF NILS
(Trans from Swedish by Velma Swanston Howard)
GIRL FROM THE MARSH CROFT
(Trans. from Swedish by Velma Swanston Howard)
LEGEND OF THE SACRED IMAGE
(Trans from Swedish by Velma Swanston Howard)
MIRACLES OF ANTICHRIST
(Trans from Swedish by Pauline Bancroft Flach)
STORY OF GÖSTA BERLING
(Trans from Swedish by Pauline Bancroft Flach)
THE EMPEROR OF PORTUGALLIA
(Trans from Swedish by Velma Swanston Howard)
THE HOLY CITY, Jerusalem II
(Trans. from Swedish by Velma Swanston Howard)
FROM A SWEDISH HOMESTEAD
(Trans from Swedish by Jessie Brochner)
INVISIBLE LINKS
(Trans from Swedish by Pauline Bancroft Flach)
LILLIECRONA'S HOME
(Trans from Swedish by Anna Barwell)
THE OUTCAST
(Trans from Swedish by W Worster, M A)
MÅRBACKA
(Trans from Swedish by Velma Swanston Howard)
THE TREASURE
(Trans from Swedish by Arthur G Chater)
CHARLOTTE LÖWENSKOLD
(Trans from Swedish by Velma Swanston Howard)

"HE GRABBED THE BOY AND TOSSED HIM . . . INTO THE AIR"

THE WONDERFUL ADVENTURES OF NILS

FROM THE SWEDISH OF
SELMA LAGERLÖF

TRANSLATED AND EDITED BY
VELMA SWANSTON HOWARD

ILLUSTRATED BY
MARY HAMILTON FRYE

Junior Books
DOUBLEDAY, DORAN & COMPANY, INC.
GARDEN CITY, NEW YORK
1936

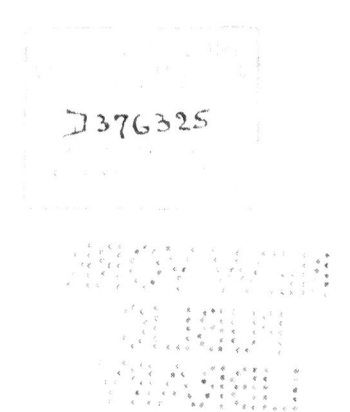

PRINTED AT THE *Country Life Press*, GARDEN CITY, N. Y., U. S. A.

COPYRIGHT, 1907, 1913
BY DOUBLEDAY, PAGE & COMPANY
ALL RIGHTS RESERVED

PUBLISHERS' NOTE

"THE Wonderful Adventures of Nils" was written for use in schools as "supplementary reading," with the special idea of introducing such subjects as would be educative as well as entertaining to the minds of children from the ages of nine to eleven. The book has been adopted in the public schools of Sweden, but older people have found in it a book of permanent value.

In so far as possible, the translator has faithfully interpreted the author's local and idiomatic expressions.

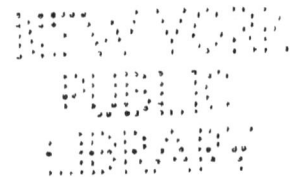

CONTENTS

CHAPTER		PAGE
	TRANSLATOR'S INTRODUCTION	xi
I.	THE BOY	3
	The Elf	
	The Wild Geese	
	The Big Checked Cloth	
II.	AKKA FROM KEBNEKAISE	24
	Evening	
	Night	
	The Goose-Chase	
III.	THE WONDERFUL JOURNEY OF NILS	45
	On the Farm	
	Vittskovle	
	In Övid Cloister-Park	
IV.	GLIMMINGE CASTLE	69
	Black Rats and Gray Rats	
	The Stork	
V.	THE GREAT CRANE DANCE ON KULLABERG	85
VI.	IN RAINY WEATHER	97
VII.	THE STAIRWAY WITH THE THREE STEPS	105
VIII.	BY RONNEBY RIVER	110
IX.	KARLSKRONA	122
X.	THE TRIP TO ÖLAND	133
XI.	ÖLAND'S SOUTHERN POINT	139
XII.	THE BIG BUTTERFLY	149

CONTENTS

CHAPTER		PAGE
XIII.	LITTLE KARL'S ISLAND	154
	The Storm	
	The Sheep	
	Hell's Hole	
XIV.	TWO CITIES	169
	The City at the Bottom of the Sea	
	The Living City	
XV.	THE LEGEND OF SMÅLAND	184
XVI.	THE CROWS	191
	The Earthen Crock	
	Kidnapped by Crows	
	The Cabin	
XVII.	THE OLD PEASANT WOMAN	213
XVIII.	FROM TABERG TO HUSKVARNA	226
XIX.	THE BIG BIRD LAKE	231
	Jarro, the Wild Duck	
	The Decoy-Duck	
	The Lowering of the Lake	
XX.	ULVÅSA-LADY	250
	(The Prophecy)	
XXI.	THE HOMESPUN CLOTH	257
	GLOSSARY	262

ILLUSTRATIONS

"HE GRABBED THE BOY AND TOSSED HIM INTO THE AIR"	*Frontispiece*
	FACING PAGE
"THE ELF BEGAN TO SPEAK, AND BEGGED, OH! SO PITIFULLY, FOR HIS FREEDOM"	8
"'SHUT UP, YOU PACK!'"	12
"THE GOOSEY-GANDER GOT IN—HEAD FIRST"	28
"THAT WHICH HE BORE SQUEALED AND SQUIRMED"	48
"'I DON'T WANT TO BE HUMAN,' SAID HE"	68
"'SEALS! SEALS! SEALS!' CRIED AKKA"	154
"'IS THERE NOT ONE AMONG YOU STRONG ENOUGH TO CARRY ME ON HIS BACK?'"	200
"'YES, THAT WOULD BE SOME HELP,' SAID THE COW"	218
"DOWN IN THE ROAD STOOD OSA, THE GOOSE-GIRL, AND HER BROTHER, LITTLE MATS, LOOKING AT A TINY WOODEN SHOE"	258

TRANSLATOR'S INTRODUCTION

THIS book, which is the latest work of Sweden's greatest fiction writer, was published in Stockholm, December, 1906. It became immediately the most popular book of the year in Scandinavia.

In 1902 the author received a commission from the National Teachers' Association to write a reader for the public schools.

She devoted three years to Nature study and to familiarizing herself with animal and bird life. She has sought out hitherto unpublished folklore and legends of the different provinces. These she has ingeniously woven into her story.

The book has been translated into German and Danish, and the book reviewers of Germany and Denmark,* as well as those of Sweden, are unanimous in proclaiming this Selma Lagerlof's best work.

One reviewer has said: "Since the days of Hans Christian Andersen we have had nothing in Scandinavian juvenile literature to compare with this remarkable book." Another reviewer wrote: "Miss Lagerlof has the keen insight into animal psychology of a Rudyard Kipling.'

Stockholm's Dagblad said among other things: "The great author stands as it were in the background. The prophetess is forgotten for the voices that speak through her. It is as though the book had sprung direct from the soul of the Swedish nation."

*Note. "The Wonderful Adventures of Nils" has since been translated into French, Dutch, Russian, and Finnish, etc.

TRANSLATOR'S INTRODUCTION

Sydsvenska Dagbladet writes: "The significant thing about this book is: while one follows with breathless interest the shifting scenes and adventures, one learns many things without being conscious of it. . . . The author's imagination unfolds an almost inexhaustible wealth in invention of new and ever-changing adventures, told in such a convincing way that we almost believe them. . . . As amusement reading for the young, this book is a decided acquisition. The intimate blending of fiction and fact is so subtle that one finds it hard to distinguish where one ends and the other begins. It is a classic. . . . A masterwork."

From *Gefle Posten:* "The author is here — as always, the great story-teller, the greatest, perhaps, in Scandinavian literature since the days of Hans Christian Andersen. To children whose imaginations have been fostered by Ashbjornsen, Andersen, and 'A Thousand Nights and One,' 'The Adventures of Nils' will always be precious, as well as to those of us who are older."

From *Goteborg Posten:* "Selma Lagerlöf has given us a good lift onward. She is the one whom we, in these days, place first and foremost. . . . Among the other work which she has done for us, and for our children, she has recreated our geography. Upon Imagination's road she has sought to open the child-heart to an understanding of animals, while tactfully and playfully dropping into little knowledge-thirsty minds a comprehensive understanding of the habits and characteristics of different animals. She carries us with her . . . and shapes for us — old and young — a new childhood in tune with the thought of our time. What does she not touch upon in this wonderful book? . . . As *Mowgli*, who had the key to all the languages of the Jungle, once found his way to all his little brother and sister hearts in the great civilized world, so shall the *Thumbietot* of Swedish fairyland lead many little thirsting child-souls not only on the highways of adventure, but also upon the road of seriousness and learning."

Another critic says: "Beyond all doubt, 'The Wonderful Adventures of Nils' is one of the most noteworthy books ever published in our language. I take it, that no other nation has a book of this sort. One can make this or that comment on one and another phase of it, but as a whole it impresses one as being so masterful, so great, and so Swedish, that one lays the book down with a sense of gratitude for the privilege of reading such a thing. There is a deep undercurrent of Swedish earnestness all through this tale of Nils. It belongs to us. It is a part of us."

Ny Tid writes: "Selma Lagerlof's book contains just as much information — no, twice as much as the old readers. It acquaints the children with Sweden's nature; interests them in its bird world, both tame and wild; in its domestic and forest animals, even in its rats. It explains its vegetation. its soil, its mountain-formations, its climatic conditions. It gives you customs, superstitions, and the folklore in different sections of the country. It takes in farming industry, manors and factories, cities and peasant-cabins, and even dog-kennels. It has a word for everything; an interest in and for everything. For, mark you, this book has not been patched together by the dilettante, or by a school board committee. . . . It was written by a highly gifted, warm-hearted seer, to whom the child-nature is not a murky pool in which to fish at random, but a clear, reflecting mirror. The author has fulfilled her mission in a wholly convincing manner. She has had enough imagination and skill to blend all the dry travel and nature material into the harmonious beauty of fable. She knew how to combine the useful with the beautiful, as no pedant of the practical or the æsthetic has ever dreamed it. She has converted the absorption of knowledge into a child's game — a pleasure. Her style throughout is the simplest, the most facile for children to grasp. . . . Her utterances are hearty without being boisterous; most playful and humorous without being loquacious. Her work is a model text-book; and just, therefore, a finished work of art."

From *Göteborg Morgon Posten:* "The fame of her literary greatness goes forward without a dissenting voice; it fills her own land, and travels far and wide outside its borders. . . . Just as modestly as she points a moral, just so delicately and unobtrusively does she give information. Everything comes to you through the adventures, or through the concrete images of imagination's all-compelling form. . . . No one who has retained a particle of his child mind can escape the genuine witchery of the poesy in 'Nils.'"

A new history of literature, entitled "Frauen der Gegenwart," by Dr. Theodore Klaiber, mentions Miss Lagerlöf as the foremost woman writer of our time, and says that she is receiving the same affectionate homage for her art in other lands that has been accorded her in Sweden. Dr. Klaiber does not see in her merely "a dreaming poetess far removed from the world." He finds her too forceful and courageous for this.

"But she sees life with other eyes than do our up-to-date people. All her world becomes saga and legend. . . . More than all other modern authors, she has that all-embracing love for every thing which never wanes and never wearies," says Dr. Klaiber.

Torsten Fågelqvist, a well-known Swedish writer, ends his review of the book with these remarks: "Our guide is clear-visioned, many-sided, and maternal. She can speak all languages: the language of animals, and the language of flowers; but first and last, childhood's language. And the best of all is, that under her spell all are compelled to become children,"

VELMA SWANSTON HOWARD.

Comments translated from Swedish and German.

THE WONDERFUL ADVENTURES OF NILS

Chapter One

THE BOY

THE ELF

Sunday, March twentieth.

ONCE there was a boy. He was, let us say, something like fourteen years old; long and loose jointed and towheaded. He wasn't good for much, that boy. His chief delight was to eat and sleep, and after that he liked best to make mischief.

It was a Sunday morning and the boy's parents were getting ready for church. The boy, in his shirt sleeves, sat on the edge of the table thinking how lucky it was that both father and mother were going away so the coast would be clear for a couple of hours. "Good! Now I can take down pop's gun and fire off a shot, without anybody's meddling interference," he said to himself.

But it was almost as if father should have guessed the boy's thoughts, for just as he was on the threshold and ready to start, he stopped short, and turned toward the boy: "Since you won't come to church with mother and me," he said, "the least you can do is to read the service at home. Will you promise to do so?" "Yes, that I can do easy enough," said the boy, thinking, of course, that he wouldn't read any more than he felt like reading.

The boy thought that never had he seen his mother get around so fast. In a jiffy she was over by the book shelf, near the fireplace, taking down Luther's Commentary, which she laid upon the table, in front of the window — opened at the service for the day. She also opened the New Testament, and placed it beside the Commentary. Finally, she drew up the big armchair, which was bought at the parish auction the year before, and which, as a rule, no one but father was permitted to occupy.

The boy sat there thinking that his mother was giving herself altogether too much trouble with this spread, for he had no intention of reading more than a page or so. But now, for the second time, it was almost as if his father were able to see right through him. He walked up to the boy, and said in a severe tone: "Now remember that you are to read carefully! For when we come back, I shall question you thoroughly; and if you have skipped a single page, it will not go well with you."

"The service is fourteen pages and a half long," said his mother, piling it on, as it were. "You'll have to sit down and begin the reading at once, if you expect to get through with it."

With that they departed. And as the boy stood in the doorway, watching them, he felt that he had been caught in a trap. "There they go congratulating themselves, I suppose, in the belief that they've hit upon something so good that I'll be forced to sit and hang over the sermon the whole time that they are away," thought he.

But his father and mother were certainly not congratulating themselves upon anything of the sort; but, on the contrary, they were very much distressed. They were poor farmers, and their place was not much bigger than a garden-plot. When they first moved there, the bit of land couldn't feed more than one pig and a pair of chickens; but they were uncommonly thrifty and capable folk — and now they had both cows and geese. Things had turned out very well for them; and they would have gone to church that beautiful morning satisfied and happy, if they hadn't had their son to think of. Father complained that he was dull and lazy; he had not cared to learn anything at school, and he was such an all-around good-for-nothing that he could barely be made to tend geese. Mother could not deny that this was true; but she was most distressed because he was wild and bad: cruel to animals, and ill-willed toward human beings. "May God soften his hard heart and give him a better disposition!" said the mother, "else he will be a misfortune, both to himself and to us."

The boy stood there a long time pondering whether he should read the service or not. Finally, he came to the conclusion that this time it was best to be obedient. He seated himself in the easy chair, and began to read. But when he had been rattling away in an undertone for a little while, this mumbling seemed to have a soothing effect upon him — and he began to nod.

It was the most beautiful weather outside! It was only the twentieth of March; but the boy lived in West Vemmenhög Parish, down in Southern Skåne, where the spring was already in full swing. It was not as yet green, but fresh and budding. There was water in all the trenches, and the colt's-foot at the edge of the ditch was in bloom. All the weeds that grew in among the stones were brown and shiny. The beech-woods in the distance seemed to swell and grow thicker with every second. The skies were high, and a clear blue. The cottage door stood ajar, and the lark's trill could be heard in the room. The hens and geese pattered about in the yard; and the cows, who felt the spring air away in their stalls, lowed their approval every now and then.

The boy read and nodded and fought against drowsiness. "No! I don't want to fall asleep," thought he, "for then I'll not get through with this thing the whole forenoon."

But somehow he fell asleep.

He did not know whether he had slept a short while or a long while; but he was awakened by hearing a slight noise back of him.

On the window-sill, facing the boy, stood a small looking-glass; and almost the entire cottage could be seen in it. As the boy raised his head, he happened to look in the glass; and then he saw that the cover to his mother's chest had been opened.

His mother owned a great, heavy, iron-bound oak chest, which she permitted no one but herself to open. Here she treasured all the things she had inherited from her mother, and of these she was especially careful. Here lay a couple of old-time peasant dresses, of red homespun with short bodice and plaited skirt, and a pearl-bedecked breast-pin. There were starched white linen headdresses, and heavy silver ornaments and chains. Folks don't care to go about dressed like that in these days, and several times his mother had thought of getting rid of the old things; but somehow, she hadn't the heart to do it.

Now the boy saw distinctly — in the glass — that the chest-lid was open. He could not understand how this had happened, for his mother had closed the chest before she went. She never would have left that precious chest open with only him here.

He became low-spirited and apprehensive. He was afraid that a thief had sneaked his way into the cottage. He didn't dare move, but sat still and stared into the looking-glass.

While he sat there and waited for the thief to make his appearance, he began to wonder what that dark shadow was which fell across the edge of the chest. He stared and stared and wouldn't believe his eyes. But the object, which at first seemed shadowy, became more and more clear to him; and soon he saw that it was something real. It was nothing less than an elf that sat there — astride the edge of the chest!

To be sure, the boy had heard stories about elves, but he had never dreamed that they were such tiny creatures. He was no taller than a hand's breadth — this one, who sat on the edge of the chest. He had an old, wrinkled and beardless face, and was dressed in a black frock coat, knee-breeches and a broad-brimmed black hat. He was very trim and smart, with his white laces at the throat and wrist-bands, his buckled shoes, and the bows on his garters. He had taken from the chest an embroidered piece, and sat gazing at the old-fashioned handiwork with such an air of veneration that he did not observe the boy had awakened.

The boy was somewhat surprised to see the elf, but, on the other hand, he was not exactly frightened. It was impossible to be afraid of one who was so little. And since the elf was so absorbed in his own thoughts that he neither saw nor heard, the boy thought that it would be great fun to play a trick on him; to push him over into the chest and shut the lid on him, or something of that kind.

Yet the boy was not so courageous that he dared touch the elf with his hands, instead he glanced around the room for something to poke him with. He let his gaze wander from the sofa to the leaf-table; from the leaf-table to the fireplace. He glanced at the kettles, then at the coffee-urn, which stood on a shelf, near the fireplace; on the water bucket, near the door; and on the spoons and knives and forks and saucers and plates, which could be seen through the half-open cupboard door. He looked up at his father's gun, which hung on the wall beside the portrait of the Danish royal family, and at the geraniums and fuchsias, which blossomed in the window. And last, he caught sight of an old butterfly-snare that hung on the window frame. He had hardly set eyes on that butterfly-snare, before he reached over and snatched it and jumped up and swung it alongside the edge of the chest. He was himself astonished at the luck he had. He hardly knew how he had managed it — but he had actually snared the elf. The poor little chap lay, head downward, in the bottom of the long snare, and could not free himself.

At the first moment the boy hadn't the least idea as to what he should do with his catch; but he was very careful to swing the snare backward and forward, to prevent the elf from getting a foothold and clambering up.

The elf began to speak, and begged, oh! so pitifully, for his freedom. He had brought them good luck these many years, he said, and deserved better treatment. Now, if the boy would set him free, he would give him an old penny, a silver spoon, and a gold coin, as big as the case on his father's silver watch.

The boy didn't think that this was much of an offer; but it so happened that after he had got the elf into his power, he was afraid of him. He felt that he had entered into an agreement with something weird and uncanny, something which did not belong to his world; and he was only too glad to rid himself of the horrid creature.

"THE ELF BEGAN TO SPEAK, AND BEGGED, OH! SO PITIFULLY, FOR HIS FREEDOM"

For this reason he agreed at once to the bargain, and held the snare still, so the elf could crawl out of it. But when the elf was almost out of the snare, the boy happened to think that he should have bargained for large estates, and all sorts of good things. He should at least have made this stipulation: that the elf conjure the sermon into his head. "What a fool I was to let him go!" thought he, and began to shake the snare violently, so the elf would tumble down again.

But the instant the boy did that he received such a stinging box on the ear that he thought his head would fly in pieces. He was dashed — first against one wall, then against the other; finally he sank to the floor, and lay there — senseless.

When he awoke he was alone in the cottage. There was not a sign of the elf! The chest-lid was down, and the butterfly-snare hung in its usual place by the window. If he had not felt how the right cheek burned from that box on the ear, he would have been tempted to believe the whole thing a dream. "At any rate, father and mother will be sure to insist that it was nothing else," thought he. "They are not likely to make any allowances for that old sermon, on the elf's account. It's best for me to get at that reading again," thought he.

But as he walked toward the table, he noticed something remarkable. It couldn't be possible that the cottage had grown. But why did he have to take so many more steps than usual to get to the table? And what was wrong with the chair? It looked no bigger than it did a while ago, but now he had to step on the rung first, and then clamber up in order to reach the seat. It was the same with the table. He could not look across the top without climbing to the arm of the chair.

"What in all the world is this?" said the boy. "I believe the elf has bewitched both armchair and table — and the whole cottage."

The Commentary lay on the table and, to all appearances, it was not changed; but there must have been something queer about that too, for he could not manage to read a single word of it without actually standing right in the book itself.

He read a couple of lines, then happened to look up. With that, his glance fell on the looking-glass; and then he cried aloud: "Look! There's another one!"

For in the glass he saw plainly a little, little creature who was dressed in a hood and leather breeches.

"Why, that one is dressed exactly like me!" said the boy, clasping his hands in astonishment. And then he saw that the thing in the mirror did the same thing. Thereupon, he began to pull his hair and pinch his arms and swing round; and instantly he did the same thing after him; he, who was seen in the mirror.

The boy ran around the glass several times, to see if here wasn't a little man hidden behind it, but he found no one there; and then he began to shake with terror. For now he understood that the elf had bewitched him, and that the creature whose image he saw in the glass was — himself.

THE WILD GEESE

The boy simply could not make himself believe that he had been transformed into an elf. "It can't be anything but a dream — a queer fancy," thought he. "If I wait a few moments, I'll surely be turned back into a human being."

He placed himself before the glass and closed his eyes. He opened them again after a couple of minutes, expecting to find that it had all passed over — but it hadn't. He was — and remained — just as little. In other respects, he was the same as before. The thin, straw-coloured hair; the freckles across his nose; the patches on his leather breeches and the darns on his stockings were all like themselves, with this difference; they had become diminished.

No, it would do him no good to stand still and wait, of that he was certain. He must try something else. And he thought the wisest thing that he could do was to try to find the elf, and make his peace with him.

He jumped to the floor and began to search. He looked behind chairs and cupboards; under the sofa and in the oven, and he even crawled down into a couple of ratholes — but he simply couldn't find the elf.

And while he sought, he cried and prayed and promised everything he could think of. Nevermore would he break his word to any one; never again would he be naughty; and never, never would he fall asleep any more over the sermon. If he might only be a human being once more, he would be such a good and helpful and obedient boy. But no matter how much he promised, it did not help him the least little bit.

Suddenly he remembered that he had heard his mother say, all the tiny folk made their home in the cowshed; and, at once, he decided to go there, to see if he couldn't find the elf. It was a lucky thing that the cottage-door stood partly open, for he never could have reached the bolt and opened it; but now he slipped through without difficulty.

When he came out into the hallway, he looked around for

his wooden shoes; for in the house to be sure, he had gone about in his stocking feet. He wondered how he should ever manage with these big, clumsy wooden shoes; but just then, he happened to see a pair of tiny shoes on the doorstep. When he observed that the elf had been so thoughtful as to bewitch even the wooden shoes, he was more troubled than ever. It was evidently the elf's meaning that this affliction should last a long time.

On the old plank-walk in front of the cottage, hopped a gray sparrow. It had hardly set eyes on the boy before it called out: "Teetee! Teetee! Look at Nils goosey-boy! Look at Thumbietot! Look at Nils Holgersson Thumbietot!"

Instantly the geese and the chickens turned and stared at the boy; and then they set up a fearful cackling. "Cock-el-i-coo," crowed the rooster, "good enough for him! Cock-el-i-coo, he has pulled my comb." "Ka, ka, kada, serves him right!" cried the hens; and with that they kept up a continuous cackle. The geese got together in a tight group, stuck their heads together and asked: "Who can have done this? Who can have done this?"

But the strangest of all was, that the boy understood what they said. He was so astonished that he stood there as if rooted to the doorstep, and listened. "It must be because I am turned into an elf," said he. "This is probably why I understand bird-talk."

He thought it unbearable that the hens would not stop saying that it served him right. He threw a stone at them and shouted: "Shut up, you pack!"

But it hadn't occurred to him before that he was no longer the sort of boy the hens need fear. The whole henyard made a rush at him, and formed a ring around him; then

"SHUT UP, YOU PACK!"

they all cried at once: "Ka, ka, kada, served you right! Ka, ka, kada, served you right!"

The boy tried to get away, but the chickens ran after him and screamed until he thought he'd lose his hearing. It is more than likely that he never could have got away from them if the house cat hadn't come along just then. As soon as the chickens saw the cat, they quieted down and pretended to be thinking of nothing else than just to scratch in the earth for worms.

Immediately the boy ran up to the cat. "You dear pussy!" he said, "you must know all the corners and hiding-places hereabout? You'll be a good little kitty and tell me where I can find the elf."

The cat did not reply at once. He sat down leisurely, curled his tail into a graceful ring around his paws — and stared at the boy. It was a large black cat with one white spot on the chest. His fur lay sleek and soft, and shone in the sunlight. The claws were drawn in, and the eyes were a dull gray, with just a little narrow dark streak down the centre. The cat looked thoroughly good-natured and inoffensive.

"I know well enough where the elf lives," he said in a soft voice, "but that doesn't say that I'm going to tell *you* about it."

"Dear pussy, you must tell me where the elf lives!" pleaded the boy. "Can't you see how he has bewitched me?"

The cat opened his eyes a little, so that the green wickedness began to shine forth. He spun round and purred with satisfaction before he replied. "Shall I perhaps help you because you have so often grabbed me by the tail?" he said at last.

Then the boy was furious and forgot entirely how little and helpless he was now. "Oh! I can pull your tail again, I can," said he, and ran toward the cat.

The next instant the cat was so changed that the boy could scarcely believe it was the same animal. Every separate hair on his body stood on end. The back was bent; the legs had become elongated; the claws scraped the ground; the tail had grown thick and short; the ears were laid back; the mouth was frothy; the eyes were wide open and glistened like sparks of red fire.

The boy didn't want to let himself be scared by a cat so he took a step forward. Then the cat made one spring and landed right on the boy, knocked him down and stood over him — his forepaws on his chest, his jaws wide apart over his throat.

The boy felt how the sharp claws sank through his vest and shirt into his skin; and how the sharp eyeteeth tickled his throat. He shrieked for help as loudly as he could, but no one came. He thought surely that his last hour had come. Then he felt that the cat drew in his claws and let go the hold on his throat.

"There!" he said, "that will do for now. I'll let you go this time, for my mistress's sake. I only wanted you to know which one of us two has the power now."

With that the cat walked away, looking as smooth and pious as when he first appeared on the scene. The boy was so crestfallen that he couldn't say a word, but only hurried to the cowhouse to look for the elf.

There were not more than three cows, all told. But when the boy came in, there was such a bellowing and such a kick-up, that one might easily have believed there were at least thirty.

"Moo, moo, moo," bellowed Mayrose. "It is well there is such a thing as justice in this world."

"Moo, moo, moo," sang the three of them in unison. He couldn't hear what they said, for each tried to out-bellow the others.

The boy wanted to ask after the elf, but he couldn't make himself heard because the cows were in full uproar. They carried on as they used to when he would let a strange dog in on them. They kicked with their hind legs, shook their flanks, stretched their heads, and measured the distance with their horns.

"Come here, you!" said Mayrose, "and you'll get a kick that you won't forget in a hurry!"

"Come here," said Gold Lily, "and you shall dance on my horns!"

"Come here, and you shall taste how it felt when you threw your wooden shoes at me, as you did last summer!" bawled Star.

"Come here, and you shall be repaid for that wasp you let loose in my ear!" growled Gold Lily.

Mayrose was the oldest and wisest among them, and she was the very maddest. "Come here!" she said, "that I may pay you back for the many times that you have jerked the milk pail away from your mother, and for all the snares you laid for her when she came carrying the milk pails and for all the tears which she has stood here and wept over you!"

The boy wanted to tell them how much he regretted that he had been unkind to them; and that never, never, from now on, should he be anything but good, if they would only tell him where the elf was. But the cows didn't listen to him. They made such a racket that he began to fear one of them would succeed in breaking loose; so he thought that the best thing for him to do, was to go quietly away from the cowhouse.

When he came out again he was thoroughly disheartened. He could understand that no one on the place wanted to help him find the elf. And little good would it do him, probably, if the elf were found!

He crawled up on the broad hedge which fenced in the farm, and which was overgrown with brier and lichen. There he sat down to ponder how it would go with him, were he never again to become a human being. When father and mother got back from church, there would be a surprise for them. Yes, a surprise — it would be all over the land; and people would come flocking from East Vemmenhög, and from Torp, and from Skerup. The whole Vemmenhög Parish would come to stare at him. Perhaps father and mother would take him along to Kivik, and show him at the market-place.

No, that was too horrible to think about. He would rather that no human being should ever see him again.

His unhappiness was simply frightful! No one in all the world was so unhappy as he. He was no longer a human being — but a freak.

Little by little he began to comprehend what it meant — to be no longer human. He was separated from everything now; he could no longer play with other boys, he could not take charge of the farm after his parents were gone; and certainly no girl would think of marrying *him*.

He sat and looked at his home. It was a little log house, which lay as if crushed down to earth, under the high, sloping roof. The outhouses were also small; and the patches of tilled ground were so narrow that a horse could barely turn around on them. But little and poor though the place was, it was much too good for him *now*. He couldn't hope for a better home than a hole under the stable floor.

It was wondrously beautiful weather! It budded, and it rippled, and it murmured, and it twittered — all around him. But he sat there with such a heavy sorrow. He should never be happy any more about anything.

Never had he seen the skies so blue as they were to-day. Birds of passage were on the wing. They came from foreign lands, having travelled over the Baltic Sea by way of Smygahuk, and were now on their way north. They were of many different kinds; but he was only familiar with the wild geese, who came flying in two long lines, which met at an angle.

Several flocks of wild geese had already flown by. They flew very high, still he could hear how they shrieked: "To the hills! Now we're off to the hills!"

When the wild geese saw the tame geese who walked about the farm, they sank nearer the earth, and called: "Come along! Come along! We're off to the hills!"

The tame geese could not resist the temptation to raise their heads and listen, but they answered very sensibly: "We're pretty well off where we are. We're pretty well off where we are."

It was, as said, an uncommonly fine day, with an atmosphere that it must have been a real delight to fly in, so light and bracing. And with each new wild goose flock that flew by, the tame geese became more and more excited. A couple of times they flapped their wings, as if they had half a mind to fly along. But then an old mother-goose would always say to them: "Now don't be silly. Those creatures will have to suffer both hunger and cold."

There was a young gander whom the wild geese had fired with a passion for adventure. "If another flock comes this way I'll follow them," said he.

Then there came a new flock, shrieking like the others, and the young gander answered: "Wait a minute! Wait a minute! I'm coming."

He spread his wings and raised himself into the air; but he was so unaccustomed to flying that he fell to the ground again.

At all events, the wild geese must have heard his call, for they turned and flew back slowly to see if he was coming.

"Wait, wait!" he cried, and made another attempt to fly.

All this the boy heard, where he lay on the hedge. "It would be a great pity," thought he, "if the big gooseygander should go away. It would be a big loss to father and mother to find him gone on their return from church."

As he thought of this, once again he entirely forgot that he was little and helpless. He took one leap right down into the goose-flock, and threw his arms around the neck of the goosey-gander. "Oh, no! You don't fly away this time, sir!" cried he.

But just about then, the gander was considering how he should go to work to raise himself from the ground. He couldn't stop to shake the boy off, hence he had to go along with him — up in the air.

They bore on toward the heights so rapidly that the boy fairly gasped. Before he had time to think that he ought to let go his hold around the gander's neck, he was so high up that he would have been instantly killed, had he fallen to the ground.

The only thing that he could do to make himself a little more comfortable, was to try to get upon the gander's back. And there he wriggled himself forthwith; but not without a mighty effort. Nor was it easy to hold himself secure on the slippery back, between two flapping wings. He had to dig deep into feathers and down with both hands, to keep from tumbling to the ground.

THE BIG CHECKED CLOTH

THE boy had grown so giddy that it was a long while before he came to himself. The winds howled and lashed against him, and the rustle of feathers and beatings of wings sounded like a full storm. Thirteen geese flew around him, flapping their wings and honking. They danced before his eyes and they buzzed in his ears. He didn't know whether they flew high or low, or in which direction they were travelling.

After a bit, he regained just enough sense to understand that he ought to find out where the geese were taking him. But this was not so easy, for he didn't know how he should ever muster up courage enough to look down. He was sure he'd faint if he attempted it.

The wild geese were not flying very high because the new travelling companion could not breathe in the very thinnest air. For his sake, they also flew a little slower than usual.

At last the boy just made himself cast one glance down to earth. Then he fancied that a great big rug lay spread beneath him, which was made up of an incredible number of large and small checks.

"Where in all the world am I now?" he wondered.

He saw nothing but check upon check. Some were

broad and ran crosswise, and some were long and narrow — all over there were angles and corners. Nothing was round, and nothing was crooked.

"What kind of big, checked cloth is this, that I'm looking down on?" said the boy to himself without expecting any one to answer him.

But instantly, the wild geese who circled around him, called out: "Fields and meadows. Fields and meadows."

Then he understood that the big, checked cloth he was travelling over was the flat land of southern Sweden; and he began to comprehend why it looked so checked and multi-coloured. The bright green checks he recognized first, they were rye-fields that had been sown in the fall, and had kept themselves green under the winter snows. The yellowish-gray checks were stubble-fields — the remains of the oat-crop which had grown there the summer before. The brownish ones were old clover meadows: and the black ones, deserted grazing lands or ploughed-up fallow pastures. The brown checks with the yellow edges were surely beech-tree forests; for in these you'll find the big trees which grow in the heart of the forest, naked in winter; while the little beech-trees, which grow along the borders, keep their dry, yellowed leaves far into the spring. There were also dark checks with gray centres: these were the large, built-up estates encircled by the small cottages with their blackening straw roofs and their stone-divided landplots. And then there were checks green in the middle with brown borders: these were the orchards, where the grass-carpets were already turning green, although the trees and bushes around them were still in their nude brown bark.

The boy could not keep from laughing when he saw how checked everything looked.

But when the wild geese heard him laugh, they called out kind o' reprovingly: "Fertile and good land. Fertile and good land."

The boy had already become serious. "To think that you can laugh; you, who have met with the most terrible misfortune that can possibly befall a human being!" thought he. And for a moment he was quite solemn; but before long he was laughing again.

Now that he had grown somewhat accustomed to the ride and the speed, so that he could think of something besides holding himself on the gander's back, he began to notice how full the air was of birds flying northward. And there was a shouting and a calling from flock to flock. "So you came over to-day?" shrieked some. "Yes," answered the geese. "How do you think the spring's getting on?" "Not a leaf on the trees and ice-cold water in the lakes," came back the answer.

When the geese flew over a place where they saw tame, half-naked fowl, they shouted: "What's the name of this place? What's the name of this place?" Then the roosters cocked their heads and answered: "Its name's Lillgarde this year — the same as last year; the same as last year."

Most of the cottages were probably named after their owners, which is the custom in Skåne. But instead of saying this is "Per Matsson's," or "Ola Bosson's," the roosters hit upon the kind of names which, to their way of thinking, were more appropriate. Those who lived on small farms and belonged to poor cottagers cried: "This place is called Grainscarce." And those who belonged to the poorest hut-dwellers screamed: "The name of this place is Little-to-eat, Little-to-eat, Little-to-eat."

The big, well-cared-for farms got high-sounding names

from the roosters — such as Luckymeadow, Eggberga and Moneyville.

But the roosters on the great landed estates were too high and mighty to condescend to anything like jesting. One of them crowed and called out with such gusto that it sounded as if he wanted to be heard clear up to the sun: "This is Herr Dybeck's estate; the same this year as last year, this year as last year."

A little farther on strutted one rooster that crowed: "This is Swanholm, surely all the world knows that!"

The boy observed that the geese did not fly straight forward, but zigzagged hither and thither over the whole South country, as if they were glad to be in Skåne again and wanted to pay their respects to every single place.

They came to one place where there were a number of big, clumsy-looking buildings, with great, tall chimneys, and all around these were a lot of little houses. "This is Jordberga Sugar Refinery," crowed the roosters. The boy shuddered as he sat there on the goose's back. He should have recognized this locality, for it was not very far from his home.

Here he had worked the year before as a watch boy; but, to be sure, nothing was quite the same when seen like that — from up above.

And think! Just think! Osa the goose girl and little Mats had been his comrades last year! Indeed the boy would have been glad to know if they were still anywhere about here. Fancy what they would have said, had they suspected that he was flying over their heads!

Soon Jordberga was lost to sight, and they travelled toward Svedala and Skaber Lake and back again over Böringe Cloister and Häckeberga. The boy saw more of

Skåne in this one day than he had ever seen before in all the years that he had lived.

When the wild geese happened across any tame geese, they had the best fun! Then they flew forward very slowly and called down: "We're off to the hills. Are you coming along? Are you coming along?"

But the tame geese answered: "It's still winter in this country. You're out too soon. Fly back! Fly back!"

The wild geese flew lower that they might be heard a little better, and called: "Come along! We'll teach you how to fly and swim."

Then the tame geese got mad and wouldn't answer them with a single honk.

The wild geese sank lower and lower until they almost touched the ground — then, quick as lightning, they rose as if they'd been terribly frightened. "Oh, oh, oh!" they exclaimed. "Those creatures were not geese. They were only sheep, they were only sheep."

The ones on the ground were beside themselves with rage, and shrieked: "May you be shot, the whole lot o' you! The whole lot o' you!"

When the boy heard all this teasing he laughed. Then he remembered how badly things had gone with him, and cried. But the next second, he was laughing again.

Never before had he ridden so fast; and to ride fast and recklessly — that he had always liked. And, of course, he had never dreamed that it could be so fresh and bracing as it was up in the air; or that there arose from the earth such a fine scent of resin and soil. Nor had he ever dreamed what it would be like to ride so high above the earth. It was just like flying away from sorrow and trouble and annoyances of every kind that could be thought of.

CHAPTER TWO

AKKA FROM KEBNEKAISE

EVENING

THE big tame goosey-gander, that had followed them up in the air, felt very proud of being allowed to travel back and forth over the south country with the wild geese, and crack jokes with the tame birds. But happy as he was he began to grow tired as the afternoon wore on. He tried to take deeper breaths and quicker wing-strokes, but even so he remained several goose-lengths behind the others.

When the wild geese who flew last noticed that the tame one couldn't keep up with them, they began to call to the goose who flew in the centre of the wedge and led the procession: "Akka from Kebnekaise! Akka from Kebnekaise!" "What do you want of me?" asked the leader. "The white one will be left behind; the white one will be left behind." "Tell him it's easier to fly fast than slow!" shouted the leader, and raced on as before.

The goosey-gander certainly tried to follow the advice, and increased his speed; but soon he became so exhausted that he sank way down to the drooping willows that bordered the fields and meadows.

"Akka, Akka, Akka from Kebnekaise!" cried those who flew last and saw what a hard time he was having. "What do you want now?" asked the leader — and she sounded awfully angry. "The white one sinks to the earth; the white one sinks to the earth." "Tell him it's easier to fly high than low!" screamed the leader, and she didn't slow up the least little bit, but raced on as before.

The goosey-gander tried also to follow this advice; but when he attempted to rise, he became so winded that he almost burst his breast.

"Akka, Akka!" again cried those who flew last. "Can't you let me fly in peace?" snapped the leader, and she sounded even madder than before.

"The white one is ready to collapse." "Tell him that he who has not the strength to fly with the flock, can go back home!" cried the leader. She certainly had no notion of decreasing her speed — but raced on as before.

"Oh, is that the way the wind blows!" thought the goosey-gander. He understood at once that the wild geese had no idea of taking him along up to Lapland. They had only lured him away from home in sport.

He felt thoroughly exasperated. To think that his strength should fail him now, so he wouldn't be able to show these tramps that even a tame goose was good for something! But the most provoking of all was that he had fallen in with Akka from Kebnekaise. Tame goose that he was, he had heard about a leader goose, named Akka, who was more than a hundred years old. She had such a big name that the best wild geese in the world followed her. But none had such a contempt for tame geese as Akka and her flock, and he would gladly have shown them that he was their equal.

He flew slowly behind the rest, while deliberating whether he should turn back or continue. Finally, the little creature that he carried on his back said: "Dear Morten Goosey-gander, you know well enough that it is simply impossible for you, who have never flown, to go with the wild geese all the way up to Lapland. Won't you turn back before you kill yourself?"

But the farmer's lad was about the worst thing the goosey-gander knew of, and, as soon as it dawned on him that this puny creature actually believed that he couldn't make the trip, he decided to stick it out. "If you say another word about this, I'll drop you into the first ditch we ride over!" said he, and at the same time his fury gave him so much strength that he began to fly almost as well as any of the others.

It isn't likely that he could have kept up this speed very long, nor was it necessary; for, just then, the sun sank quickly; and at sunset the geese flew down, and before the boy or the goosey-gander knew what had happened, they stood on the shore of Vomb Lake.

"They probably intend that we shall spend the night here," thought the boy as he jumped down from the goose's back.

He stood now on a narrow beach by a fair-sized lake. It was ugly to look upon, for it was almost entirely covered with an ice-crust that was blackened and uneven and full of cracks and holes — as spring ice generally is.

The ice was already breaking up. It was loose and floating with a broad belt of dark, shiny water all around it; but there was still enough of it left to spread chill and winter terror over the place.

On the other side of the lake there appeared to be an open and light country, but where the geese had alighted there was a thick pine-growth. It looked as if the forest of firs and pines had the power to bind the winter to itself. Everywhere else the ground was bare; but beneath the sharp pine-branches lay snow that had been melting and freezing, melting and freezing, till it was as hard as ice.

The boy thought he had struck an arctic wilderness, and he was so miserable that he wanted to scream. He was hungry too. He hadn't eaten a bite the whole day. But where should he find any food? Nothing eatable grew on either ground or tree in the month of March.

Yes, where was he to find food, and who would give him shelter, and who would fix his bed, and who would protect him from the wild beasts?

For now the sun was away and frost came from the lake, and darkness sank down from heaven, and terror stole forward on the twilight's trail, and in the forest it began to patter and rustle.

Now the good humour which the boy had felt when he was up in the air was gone, and in his misery he looked around for his travelling companions. He had no one but them to cling to now.

Then he saw that the goosey-gander was having even a worse time of it. He was lying prostrate on the spot where he had alighted; and it looked as if he were ready to die. His neck lay flat against the ground, his eyes were closed, and his breathing sounded like a feeble hissing.

"Dear Morten Goosey-gander," said the boy, "try to get a swallow of water! It isn't two steps to the lake."

But the goosey-gander didn't stir.

The boy had certainly been cruel to all animals, and to the goosey-gander in times gone by; but now he felt that the goosey-gander was the only comfort he had left, and he was dreadfully afraid of losing him.

All at once the boy began to push and drag him, to get him into the water, but the goosey-gander was big and heavy, and it was mighty hard work for the boy; but at last he succeeded.

The goosey-gander got in — head first. For an instant he lay motionless in the slime, but soon he poked up his head, shook the water from his eyes, and sniffed. Then he swam proudly between reeds and seaweed.

The wild geese were in the lake before him. They had not looked around, for either the goosey-gander or his rider, but had made straight for the water. They had bathed and primped, and now they lay and gulped half-rotten pond-weed and water-clover.

The white goosey-gander had the good fortune to spy a perch. He grabbed it quickly, swam ashore with it, and laid it down in front of the boy. "Here's a thank you for helping me into the water," said he.

Those were the first friendly words the boy had heard that day. He was so happy that he wanted to throw his arms around the goosey-gander's neck, but he didn't; and he was also thankful for the gift. At first he thought it would be impossible for him to eat raw fish, and then he had a notion to try it.

He felt to see if he still had his sheath-knife with him; and, sure enough, there it hung — on the back button of his trousers, although it was so diminished that it was hardly as long as a match. Well, at any rate, it served to scale and cleanse fish with; and it wasn't long before the perch was eaten.

When the boy had satisfied his hunger, he felt a little ashamed because he had been able to eat a raw animal. "It's evident that I'm no longer a human being but a real elf," thought he.

While the boy was eating, the goosey-gander stood

"THE GOOSEY-GANDER GOT IN — HEAD FIRST"

quietly beside him. But when he had swallowed the last morsel he said in a low voice: "It's a fact that we have run across a stuck-up goose folk who despise all tame birds."

"Yes, I've observed that," said the boy.

"What a triumph it would be for me if I could follow them clear up to Lapland, and show them that even a tame goose can do things!"

"Y-e-e-s," said the boy, drawling it out, for he didn't believe the goosey-gander could ever do it; yet he did not wish to contradict him. "But I don't think I can get along all by myself on such a journey," said the goosey-gander. "I'd like to ask if you couldn't come along to help me?" The boy, of course, hadn't expected anything but to return to his home as soon as possible, and he was so surprised that he hardly knew what he should reply. "I thought that we were enemies, you and I," said he. But this the goosey-gander seemed to have forgotten entirely. He only remembered that the boy had but just saved his life.

"I suppose I really ought to go home to father and mother," said the boy. "Oh, I'll get you back to them some time in the fall," assured the goosey-gander. "I shall not leave you until I can set you down on your own doorstep."

The boy thought it would be just as well for him not to be seen by his parents yet a while. He was not disinclined to favour the proposition, and was just on the point of saying that he agreed to it — when they heard a loud rumbling from behind. The wild geese had just come up from the lake — all at one time — and stood shaking the water from their backs. After that, they arranged themselves in a long row with the leader-goose in the centre — and came toward them.

As the white goosey-gander sized up the wild geese, he felt ill at ease. He had expected that they should be more like tame geese, and that he should feel a closer kinship with them. They were much smaller than he, and none of them was white. All were gray with a sprinkling of brown. He was almost afraid of their eyes, which were yellow and shone as if a fire had been kindled back of them. The goosey-gander had always been taught that it was most fitting to move slowly and with a rolling motion, but these creatures did not walk — they almost ran. He grew most alarmed, however, when he looked at their feet. They were large, with torn and ragged-looking soles. It was apparent that the wild geese never questioned what they tramped upon. They took no by-paths. They were very neat and well cared for in other respects, but one could tell by their feet that they were poor wilderness-folk.

The goosey-gander only had time to whisper to the boy: "Speak up quickly for yourself, but don't tell them who you are!" — before the geese were upon them.

When the wild geese had stopped in front of them, they courtesied with their necks many times, and the goosey-gander did likewise many more times. As soon as the ceremonies were over, the leader-goose said: "Now I presume we shall hear what kind of creatures you are."

"There isn't much to tell about me," said the goosey-gander. "I was born in Skanör last spring. In the fall I was sold to Holger Nilsson of West Vemmenhög, and there I have lived ever since." "You don't seem to have any pedigree to boast of," said the leader-goose. "What is it, then, that makes you so high-minded that you wish to associate with wild geese?" "It may be because I want to show you wild geese that we tame ones may also be good for something," said the goosey-gander. "Yes, it would be well if you could show us that," challenged the leader-goose. "We have already observed how much you know about flying; but you are more skilled, perhaps, at other sports. Possibly you are strong in a swimming match?" "No, I can't boast that I am," said the goosey-gander. It seemed to him as if the leader-goose had already made up her mind to send him home, so he didn't much care how he answered. "I never swam any farther than across a marl-ditch," he retorted. "Then I presume you're a crack sprinter," said the goose. "I have never seen a tame goose run, nor have I ever done so myself," said the goosey-gander; and he made things appear much worse than they really were.

The big white one was sure now that the leader-goose would say that under no circumstances could they take him along. He was very much astonished when she said: "You answer questions courageously; and he who has courage can become a good travelling companion, even if he is ignorant in the beginning. What do you say to stopping with us a couple of days, until we can see what you are good for?" "That suits me!" said the goosey-gander — and he was thoroughly happy.

Thereupon the leader-goose pointed with her bill and said: "But whom have you there? I've never seen any one like him before." "That's my comrade," said the goosey-gander. "He's been a goose-tender all his life. He'll be useful, all right, to take with us on the trip." "Yes, he may be all right for a tame goose," retorted the wild one. "What do you call him?" "He has several names," said the goosey-gander hesitatingly, not knowing what he should hit upon in a hurry, for he didn't want to reveal the fact that the boy had a human name. "Oh! his name is Thumbietot," he said at last. "Does he belong to the elf family?" asked the leader-goose. "At what hour do you wild geese usually retire?" said the goosey-gander quickly — trying to evade that last question. "My eyes close of their own accord about this time."

One could easily see that the goose who talked with the gander was very old. Her entire feather outfit was ice-gray with no dark streaks. The head was larger than that of the others; the legs were coarser, and the feet were more worn. The feathers were stiff; the shoulders knotty; the neck thin. All this was due to age. It was only upon the eyes that time had had no effect. They shone brighter — as if they were younger than those of the others.

She turned very haughtily toward the goosey-gander. "Understand, Mr. Tame-goose, that I am Akka from Kebnekaise! And that the goose who flies nearest me — to the right — is Iksi from Vassijaure, and the one to the left is Kaksi from Nuolja! Understand, also, that the second right-hand goose is Kolmi from Sarjektjakko, and the second, left, is Neljä from Svappavaara; and behind them fly Viisi from Oviksfjällen and Kuusi from Sjangeli! And know that these, as well as the six goslings, who fly last — three to the right, and three to the left — are all high mountain geese of the finest breed! You must not take us for land-lubbers who strike up a chance acquaintance with any and every one! And you must not think that we permit any one to share our quarters that will not tell us who his ancestors were."

While Akka, the leader-goose, was talking in this strain, the boy stepped briskly forward. It distressed him that the goosey-gander, who had spoken up so glibly for himself, should give such evasive answers when it concerned him. "I don't care to make a secret of who I am," said he. "My name is Nils Holgersson. I'm a farmer's son, and, until to-day, I was a human being; but this morning ——" He got no further. As soon as he said that he was human the leader-goose staggered three steps backward, and the rest of them even farther back. All craned their necks and hissed angrily at him.

"I have suspected this ever since I first saw you here on these shores," said Akka; "and now you can clear out of here at once. We tolerate no human beings among us."

"It isn't possible," said the goosey-gander, meditatively, "that you wild geese can be afraid of any one who is so tiny! By to-morrow, of course, he'll turn back home. You can surely let him stay with us overnight. None of us can afford to let such a poor little creature wander off by himself in the night — among weasels and foxes!"

The wild goose came nearer. But one could see that it was hard for her to master her fear. "I have been taught to fear everything in human shape — be it big or little," said she. "But if you will answer for this one, and swear that he will not harm us, he may stay with us to-night. But I don't believe our night quarters are suitable for either him or you, for we intend to roost on the broken ice out here."

She thought, of course, that the goosey-gander would be doubtful when he heard this, but he never let on. "She is pretty wise who knows how to choose such a safe bed," said he.

"You will be answerable for his return to his own to-morrow."

"Then I, too, will have to leave you," said the goosey-gander. "I have sworn that I would not forsake him."

"You are free to fly whither you will," said the leader-goose.

With this, she raised her wings and flew out over the ice, and, one after another, the wild geese followed her.

The boy was very sad to think that his trip to Lapland would not come off, and, in the bargain, he was afraid of the chilly night quarter. "It will be worse and worse," said he. "In the first place, we'll freeze to death on the ice."

But the gander was in good humour. "There's no danger," he said. "Only make haste, I beg of you, and gather up as much grass and litter as you can well carry."

When the boy had an armful of dried grass, the goosey-gander grabbed him by the shirt-band, lifted him, and flew out upon the ice, where the wild geese were already fast asleep with their bills tucked under their wings.

"Now spread out the grass on the ice so there will be something to stand on, to keep me from freezing fast. You help me and I'll help you," said the goosey-gander.

This the boy did. And when he had finished, the goosey-gander again picked him up by the shirt-band, and tucked him under his wing. "I think you'll lie snug and warm there," said the goosey-gander as he covered him with his wing.

The boy was so imbedded in down that he couldn't answer; and he was nice and comfy. Oh, but he was tired! And in less than two winks he was fast asleep.

NIGHT

IT is a fact that ice is always treacherous and not to be trusted. In the middle of the night the loosened ice-cake on Vomb Lake moved about, till one corner of it touched the shore. Now it happened that Mr. Smirre Fox, who lived at this time in Övid Cloister-Park — on the east side of the lake — caught a glimpse of that one corner while out on his night chase. Smirre had seen the wild geese early in the evening, and hadn't even dared to hope that he might get at one of them; but now he walked straight out on the ice.

When Smirre was very near to the geese, his claws scraped the ice, and the geese awoke, flapped their wings, and prepared for flight. But Smirre was too quick for them. He darted forward as though he'd been shot, grabbed a goose by the wing and ran toward land again.

But this night the wild geese were not alone on the ice, for they had a human being among them — little as he was. The boy had awakened when the goosey-gander spread his wings. He had tumbled down on the ice and was sitting there, dazed. He hadn't grasped the whys and wherefores of all this confusion until he had caught sight of a little long-legged dog who ran over the ice with a goose in his mouth.

In a second the boy was after that dog, to take the goose away from him. He must have heard the goosey-gander call to him: "Have a care, Thumbietot! Have a care!" But the boy thought that such a little runt of a dog was nothing to be afraid of, so he rushed ahead.

The wild goose that Smirre Fox was tugging along heard the clatter as the boy's wooden shoes beat against the ice, and she could hardly believe her ears. "Does that infant think he can take me away from the fox?" she wondered. And in spite of her misery, she began to cackle right merrily, deep down in her windpipe. It was almost as if she had laughed.

"The first thing he knows, he'll fall through a crack in the ice," thought she.

But dark as the night was, the boy saw distinctly all the cracks and holes there were, and took daring leaps over them. This was because he had the elf's good eyesight now, and could see in the dark. He saw both lake and shore just as clearly as if it had been daylight.

Smirre Fox left the ice where it touched the shore. And just as he was working his way up to the land-edge, the boy shouted to him: "Drop that goose, you sneak!" Smirre didn't know who was calling to him, and wasted no time in looking around, but increased his pace.

The fox made straight for the forest and the boy followed him, with never a thought of the risk he was running. On the contrary, he was thinking all the while about the contemptuous way in which he had been received by the wild geese that evening; and he made up his mind to let them see that a human being was something higher than all else created.

He shouted, again and again to that dog, to make him drop his game. "What kind of a dog are you, who can steal a whole goose and not feel ashamed of yourself? Drop her at once! or you'll see what a beating you'll get. Drop her, I say, or I'll tell your master how you behave!"

When Smirre Fox saw that he had been mistaken for a scary dog, he was so amused that he came near dropping the goose. Smirre was a great plunderer who wasn't satisfied with hunting only rats and pigeons in the fields, but he also ventured into the farmyards to steal chickens and geese. He knew that he was feared throughout the district; and anything so idiotic as this he had not heard since he was a baby.

The boy ran so fast that the thick beech-trees appeared to be running past him — backward, and he gained on Smirre. Finally, he was so close to him that he got a hold on his tail. "Now I'll take the goose from you anyway," cried he, holding on as tight as ever he could, but he hadn't strength enough to stop Smirre. The fox dragged him along until the dry foliage whirled around him.

But now it began to dawn on Smirre how harmless was the creature that pursued him. He stopped short, put the goose on the ground, and held her down with his forepaws, so she couldn't fly away. He was just about to bite off her neck — but he couldn't resist the desire to tease the boy a little. "Hurry off and complain to the master, for now I'm going to bite the goose to death!" said he.

Certainly the one who was surprised when he saw what a pointed nose, and heard what a hoarse and angry voice that dog which he was pursuing had, was — the boy! But now he was so provoked because the fox had made fun of him that he never thought of being frightened. He took a firmer hold on the tail, braced himself against a beech trunk; and just as the fox opened his jaws over the goose's throat, he pulled as hard as he could. Smirre was so astonished that he let himself be pulled backward a couple of steps — and the wild goose got away. She fluttered upward, feebly and heavily. One wing was so badly wounded that she could barely use it. Besides, she could not see in the night darkness of the forest, but was as helpless as the blind. Therefore she could in no way help the boy. She groped her way through the branches and flew down to the lake again.

Then Smirre made a dash for the boy. "If I don't get the one, I shall certainly have the other," said he; and you could tell by his voice how mad he was. "Oh, don't you believe it!" said the boy, who was in the best of spirits because he had saved the goose. He held himself fast by the fox-tail, and swung with it to one side when the fox tried to catch him.

There was such a dance in that forest that the dry beech-leaves fairly flew! Smirre swung round and round, but the tail swung too; while the boy kept a tight grip on it, so the fox couldn't grab him.

The boy was so gay after his success that, in the beginning, he only laughed and made fun of the fox. But Smirre was persevering — as old hunters generally are — and the boy began to fear that he would be captured in the end.

Then he caught sight of a little, young beech-tree that had shot up as slender as a rod, that it might soon reach the free air above the canopy of branches which the old beeches spread over it.

Quick as a flash, he let go of the fox-tail and climbed the beech-tree. Smirre Fox was so excited that he continued to dance around after his tail a long time.

"Don't bother with the dance any longer!" said the boy.

But Smirre couldn't endure the humiliation of his failure to get the better of such a little tot, so he laid down under the tree, that he might keep a close watch on him.

The boy didn't have any too good a time of it where he sat, astride a frail branch. The young beech did not, as yet, reach the high branch-canopy, so the boy couldn't get over to another tree, and he didn't dare come down. He was so cold and numb that he almost lost his hold around the branch; and he was dreadfully sleepy; but he didn't dare fall asleep for fear of tumbling down.

My! but it was dismal to sit in that way the whole night

through, out in the forest! He had never before understood the real meaning of "night." It was just as if the whole world had become petrified, and never could come to life again.

Then it commenced to dawn. The boy was glad that everything began to look like itself once more; although the chill was even sharper than it had been during the night.

When the sun finally came up, it wasn't yellow but red. The boy thought it looked as if it was angry and he wondered what it was angry about. Perhaps it was because the night had made it so cold and gloomy on earth while the sun was away.

The sunbeams came down in great clusters, to see what the night had been up to. It could be seen how all things blushed — as if they all had guilty consciences. The clouds in the skies; the satiny beech-limbs; the little intertwined branches of the forest-canopy; the hoar-frost that covered the brushwood — everything grew flushed and red. More and more sunbeams came bursting through space, and soon the night's terrors were driven away, and such a marvellous lot of living things came forward. The black woodpecker, with the red neck, began to hammer with its bill on the branch. The squirrel glided from his nest with a nut, sat down on a branch and began to shell it. The starling came flying with a worm, and the bullfinch sang in the tree-top.

Then the boy understood that the sun had said to all these tiny creatures: "Wake up now, and come out of your nests! I'm here! Now you needn't be afraid of anything."

The wild-goose call was heard from the lake, as the geese were preparing for flight; and soon all the fourteen geese came flying through the forest. The boy tried to call to them, but they flew so high that his voice couldn't reach them. They probably believed the fox had eaten him up; and they didn't trouble themselves to look for him.

The boy came near crying with chagrin; but the sun stood up there — orange-coloured and happy — and put courage into the whole world. "It isn't worth while, Nils Holgersson, for you to be troubled about anything, so long as I'm here," said the sun.

THE GOOSE-CHASE

Monday, March twenty-first.

EVERYTHING remained unchanged in the forest about as long as it takes a goose to eat her breakfast. But just as the morning was verging on forenoon, a goose came flying, all by herself, under the thick tree-canopy. She groped her way hesitatingly between stems and branches, and flew very slowly. As soon as Smirre Fox saw her, he left his place under the beech-tree, and sneaked toward her. The wild goose didn't avoid the fox, but flew quite close to him. Smirre made a high jump for her but missed her; and the goose went on her way, down to the lake.

It was not long until another goose came flying. She took the same route as the first one, and flew still lower and slower. She, too, flew close to Smirre Fox, and he made such a high spring for her that his ears brushed her feet. But she, too, got away from him unhurt, and went her way toward the lake, silent as a shadow.

A little while passed, and then along came another wild goose. She flew still slower and lower; and it seemed even more difficult for her to find her way between the beech-branches. Smirre made a powerful spring! He was within a hair's breadth of catching her; but that goose also managed to save herself.

Just after she had disappeared, there came a fourth. She flew so slowly and so badly, that Smirre Fox thought he could catch her without much effort, but now he was afraid of failure and decided to let her fly past, unmolested. She took the same direction the others had taken; and just as she was right above Smirre, she sank down so far that he was tempted to jump for her. He jumped so high that he touched her with his tail. But she flung herself quickly to one side, and saved her life.

Before Smirre was through panting, three more geese came flying in a row. They flew just like the rest, and Smirre made high springs for all three, but he did not succeed in catching one of them.

After that came five more geese; but these flew better than the others. And although it appeared as if they wanted to coax Smirre to jump, he withstood the temptation. After quite a long time came one lone goose. It was the thirteenth. This one was so old that she was gray all over, without a dark speck anywhere on her body. Apparently, she could use only one wing, for she flew so wretchedly and crookedly that she almost touched the ground. Smirre not only made a high leap for her, but he also pursued her, running and jumping all the way down to the lake. But not even this time did he get anything for his trouble.

When the fourteenth goose came along, it looked very pretty because it was white. And as the great wings moved, it glistened like a light in the dark forest. When Smirre Fox saw this one, he mustered all his strength and jumped halfway up to the tree-canopy. But the white one flew by unhurt like the rest.

Now it was quiet for a moment under the beeches. It looked as if the whole wild-goose flock had flown past.

Suddenly Smirre remembered his prisoner and raised his eyes toward the young beech-tree. And just as he might have expected — the boy had disappeared.

But Smirre didn't have much time to think about him; for now the first goose came back again from the lake and flew slowly under the canopy. In spite of all his bad luck, Smirre was glad that she had come back, and darted after her with high leaps. But he had been in too much of a hurry, and hadn't taken time to calculate the distance, so he landed at the side of the goose. Then there came still another goose; then a third; a fourth; a fifth; and so on, until the wedge closed in with the old ice-gray one, and the big white one. They all flew low and slow. Just as they circled in the vicinity of Smirre Fox, they sank down — kind of inviting-like — for him to take them. Smirre ran after them and made leaps a couple of metres high, but he couldn't manage to get hold of a single one of them.

It was the most awful day that Smirre Fox had ever experienced. The wild geese kept right on travelling over his head. They came and went — came and went. Great, splendid geese, who had eaten themselves fat on the German heaths and grain fields, circled all day through the woods, and so close to him that he touched them many times; yet he was not allowed to appease his hunger with a single one.

The winter was hardly gone and Smirre recalled nights

and days when he had been forced to tramp around in idleness, with not so much as a hare to hunt; when the rats hid themselves under the frozen earth; and when all the chickens were shut up. But all the winter's hunger had not been as hard to endure as this day's miscalculations.

Smirre was no young fox. He had had the dogs after him many a time, and had heard the bullets whiz around his ears. He had lain in hiding, down in the lair, while the dachshunds crept into the crevices and all but found him. But all the anguish that Smirre Fox had been forced to suffer under that hot chase was as nothing in comparison with what he suffered every time that he missed one of the wild geese.

In the morning, when the chase began, Smirre Fox looked so stunning that the geese were amazed when they saw him. Smirre loved display. His coat was a brilliant red; his breast white; his nose black; and his tail was as bushy as a plume. But when the even of this day was come, Smirre's coat hung in loose folds. He was bathed in sweat; his eyes were without lustre; his tongue hung far out from his gaping jaws; and froth oozed from his mouth.

Even in the afternoon Smirre was already so exhausted that he grew delirious. He saw nothing before his eyes but flying geese. He made leaps for sun-spots which he saw on the ground; and for a poor little butterfly that had come out of its chrysalis too soon.

The wild geese flew and flew, unceasingly. All day long they continued to torment Smirre. They were not moved to pity because Smirre was spent, fevered, and out of his head. They continued without a let-up, although they understood that he hardly saw them, and that he jumped after their shadows.

When Smirre Fox finally sank down on a pile of dry leaves, weak and powerless and almost ready to give up the ghost, they stopped teasing him.

"Now you know, Mr. Fox, what happens to the one who dares to come near Akka of Kebnekaise!" they shouted in his ear; and with that they left him in peace.

CHAPTER THREE

THE WONDERFUL JOURNEY OF NILS

ON THE FARM

Thursday, March twenty-fourth.

JUST at that time a thing happened in Skåne which created a good deal of discussion and which even got into the newspapers, but which many believed to be only a fable, because they were not able to explain it.

It was about like this: A lady squirrel had been captured in the hazelbrush along the shores of Vomb Lake, and carried to a farmhouse close by. All the folks on the farm, both young and old, were delighted with the pretty creature with the bushy tail, the wise, inquisitive eyes, and the natty little feet. They were going to amuse themselves all summer watching its nimble movements, its ingenious way of shelling nuts, and its droll play. They immediately made ready an old squirrel-cage, with a little green house and a wire cylinder-wheel. The little house, which had both doors and windows, the lady squirrel was to use as a dining-room and bedroom. Therefore they placed therein a bed of leaves, a bowl of milk, and some nuts. The cylinder-wheel she was to use as a playhouse, where she could run and climb and swing round.

The people thought they had arranged things very comfortably for the lady squirrel, and they were astonished because she didn't seem to be contented; but, instead, sat there, downcast and moody, in a corner of her room. Every now and again, she would let out a shrill, agonized cry. She did not touch the food; and not once did she swing round on the wheel. "It's probably because she's frightened," said the farmer folk. "To-morrow, when she feels more at home, she will both eat and play."

Meanwhile, the women folk on the farm were making preparation for a feast; and the very day the lady squirrel was captured, they were busy with an elaborate bake. They had had bad luck with something: either the dough wouldn't rise, or they had been dilatory, for they were obliged to work till long after dark.

Naturally there was a great deal of excitement and bustle in the kitchen, and probably no one there took time to think about the squirrel, or to wonder how she was faring. But there was an old grandma in the house who was too aged to take a hand in the baking; this she herself understood, but, all the same she did not relish the idea of being left out of the game. She felt rather downhearted; therefore she did not go to bed but seated herself by the sitting-room window to look out.

They had opened the kitchen door on account of the heat; and through it a clear ray of light streamed into the yard, which made it so light out there that the old woman could see all the cracks and holes in the plastering on the wall opposite. She also saw the squirrel-cage, which hung just where the light fell clearest. And she noticed how the squirrel ran from her room to the wheel, and from the wheel to her room, all night long, without stopping an instant. She thought it a strange sort of unrest that had come over the animal; but she believed, of course, that the strong light kept it awake.

Between the cowhouse and the stable there was a broad covered carriage-gate; this too came within the light-radius. As the night wore on, the old grandma saw a tiny creature, no bigger than a hand's breadth, cautiously stealing his way through the gate. He was dressed in leather breeches and wooden shoes, like any other workingman. The old grandma knew at once that it was the elf, and she was not the least bit frightened. She had always heard that the elf kept himself somewhere about the place, although she had never seen him before; and an elf, to be sure, brought good luck wherever he appeared.

As soon as the elf came into the stone-paved yard, he ran straight up to the squirrel-cage. And since it hung so high that he could not reach it, he went over to the storehouse after a rod; placed it against the cage, and swung himself up — in the same way that a sailor climbs a rope. When he had reached the cage, he shook the door of the little green house as if to open it; but the old grandma didn't move; for she knew that the children had put a padlock on the door, as they feared that the boys from the neighbouring farms would try to steal the squirrel. The old woman saw that when the boy could not get the door open the lady squirrel came out to the wire wheel, where they held a long conference. And when the boy had listened to all that the imprisoned animal had to say to him, he slid down the rod to the ground, and ran out through the carriage-gate.

The old woman didn't expect to see anything more of the elf that night, nevertheless, she remained at the window. In a few moments he returned. He was in such a hurry that it seemed to her as if his feet hardly touched the ground; and he rushed right over to the squirrel-cage. The old woman, with her far-sighted eyes, saw him distinctly; and she also saw that he carried something in his hands; but what it was she couldn't imagine. That which he carried in his left hand he laid down on the pavement; but that which he held in his right hand he took with him to the cage. He kicked so hard with his wooden shoes on the little window that the glass broke. And he pushed toward the lady squirrel that which he held in his hand. Then he slid down, took up what he had laid upon the ground, and climbed to the cage with that also. The next instant he ran off again with such haste that the old woman could hardly follow him with her eyes.

But now the old grandma could no longer sit still in the cottage, but very slowly went out to the backyard and stationed herself in the shadow of the pump, to await the elf's return. And there was another who had also seen him and had become curious. This was the house cat. He crept along slyly, and stopped close to the wall, just two steps away from the stream of light. The two of them stood waiting long and patiently, on that chilly March night, and the old woman was just beginning to think about going in again when she heard a clatter on the pavement, and saw the little mite of an elf come trotting along once more, carrying a burden in each hand, as he had done before. That which he bore squealed and squirmed. And now a light dawned on the old grandma. She understood that the elf had hurried down to the hazel-grove and had brought back the lady squirrel's babies, and that he was carrying them to her so they shouldn't starve to death.

The old grandma stood very still, so as not to disturb them; and it appeared as if the elf had not noticed her. He was just about to lay one of the babies on the ground so that

"THAT WHICH HE BORE SQUEALED AND SQUIRMED"

he could swing himself up to the cage with the other one — when he saw the house cat's green eyes glisten close beside him. He stood there, bewildered, with a young one in each hand.

He turned and looked in all directions; presently he became aware of the old grandma's presence. He did not hesitate long but walked forward, stretched his arms as high as he could reach for her to take one of the baby squirrels.

The old grandma did not wish to prove herself unworthy of the confidence, so she bent down and took the baby squirrel and stood there and held it until the boy had swung himself up to the cage with the other one. Then he came back for the one he had entrusted to her care.

The next morning, when the farm folk came together for breakfast, it was impossible for the old woman to refrain from telling them of what she had seen the night before. They all laughed at her, of course, and said that she had been only dreaming. There were no baby squirrels this early in the year.

But she was sure of her ground, and begged them to take a look into the squirrel-cage, which they did. And there, on the bed of leaves, lay four tiny half-naked, half-blind baby squirrels, who were at least two days old.

When the farmer himself saw the young ones, he said: "Be it as it may with this; but one thing is certain, we, on this farm, have behaved in such a manner that we are shamed before both animals and human beings." And, thereupon, he took the mother squirrel and all her young ones from the cage, and laid them in the old grandma's lap. "Go thou out to the hazel-grove with them," said he, "and let them have their freedom back again!"

It was this event that was so much talked about, and which even got into the newspapers, but which the majority would not credit because they were not able to explain how anything like that could have happened.

VITTSKÖVLE

Saturday, March twenty-sixth.
Two days later, another strange thing happened. A flock of wild geese came flying one morning, and lit on a meadow down in Eastern Skåne not very far from Vittskövle Manor. In the flock were thirteen wild geese of the usual gray variety, and one white goosey-gander, who carried on his back a tiny lad dressed in yellow leather breeches, green vest, and a white woollen toboggan hood.

They were now very near the Baltic Sea; and on the meadow where the geese had alighted the soil was sandy, as it usually is on the seacoast. It looked as if, formerly, there had been flying sand in this vicinity which had to be held down; for in several directions large, planted pine-woods could be seen.

When the wild geese had been feeding a while, some children came walking along at the edge of the meadow. The goose on guard at once rose into the air with noisy wing-strokes, so the whole flock should hear that there was danger afoot. All the wild geese flew upward; but the white one waddled along on the ground unconcerned. When he saw the others flying he raised his head and called after them: "You needn't fly away from these! They are only a couple of children!"

The little creature, who had been riding on his back, sat down upon a knoll on the outskirts of the wood and picked a pine-cone to pieces, that he might get at the seeds. The children were so close to him that he did not dare run across the meadow to the white one, but concealed himself under a big, dry thistle-leaf, and at the same time he gave a warning cry. The white one had evidently made up his mind not to let himself be scared. He waddled along on the ground all the while; and not once did he look to see in which direction they were going.

Meanwhile, they turned from the path and walked across the field, getting nearer and nearer the goosey-gander. When he finally did look up, they were right upon him. He was so dumbfounded, and became so confused that he forgot that he could fly, and tried to get out of their reach by running. But the children followed, chasing him into a ditch, where they caught him. The larger of the two children stuck him under his arm and carried him off.

When the boy, who lay under the thistle-leaf, saw this, he sprang up as if to take the goosey-gander away from them; then he must have remembered how little and powerless he was, for he threw himself on the knoll and beat the ground with his clenched fists.

The goosey-gander cried with all his might for help: "Thumbietot, come and help me! Oh, Thumbietot, come and help me!" The boy began to laugh in the midst of his distress. "Oh, yes! I'm just the right one to help anybody, I am!" said he.

Anyhow he got up and followed the goosey-gander. "I can't help him," he said, "but I shall at least find out where they are taking him."

The children had a good start; but the boy had no difficulty in keeping them within sight until they came to a hollow where a brook gushed forth. But here he was obliged to run alongside it for some little time, before he could find a place narrow enough for him to jump over.

When he came up from the hollow the children had disappeared. He could see their footprints on a narrow path which led to the woods, and these he continued to follow.

Soon he came to a crossroad. Here the children must have separated, for there were footprints in two directions. The boy looked now as if all hope had fled. Then he saw a little white down on a heather-knoll, and understood that the goosey-gander had dropped this by the wayside to let him know in which direction he had been carried; and therefore he continued his search. He followed the children through the entire wood. The goosey-gander he did not see; but wherever he was likely to miss his way, lay a little white down to put him right.

The boy continued faithfully to follow the bits of down. They led him out of the wood, across a couple of meadows, into a road, and finally through the entrance of a broad avenue. At the end of the avenue there were gables and towers of red tiling, decorated with bright borders and other ornamentations that glittered and shone. When the boy saw that this was some great manor, he thought he knew what had become of the goosey-gander. "No doubt the children have carried the goosey-gander to the manor and sold him there. By this time he's probably butchered," he said to himself. But he did not seem to be satisfied with anything less than proof positive, and with renewed courage he ran forward. He met no one in the avenue — and that was well, for such as he are generally afraid of being seen by human beings.

The mansion which he came to was a splendid, old-time structure with four great wings which inclosed a courtyard.

On the east wing, there was a high arch leading into the courtyard. Thus far the boy had run without hesitation, but when he was there he stopped. He dared not venture farther, but stood still and pondered what he should do next.

There he stood, with his finger on his nose, thinking, when he heard footsteps behind him; and as he turned around he saw a whole company march up the avenue. Hastily he stole behind a water-barrel which stood near the arch, and hid himself.

Those who came up were some twenty young men from a folk high-school, out on a pedestrian tour. They were accompanied by one of the instructors. When they were come as far as the arch, the teacher requested them to wait there a moment, while he went in and asked if they might see the old castle of Vittskövle.

The newcomers were warm and tired, as if they had been on a long tramp. One of them was so thirsty that he went over to the water-barrel and bent down to drink. He had a tin box, such as botanists use, suspended from his neck. He evidently thought it was in his way, for he threw it down on the ground. With that the lid flew open, and one could see that there were a few spring flowers inside.

The botanist's tin dropped just in front of the boy; and he saw that here was his opportunity to get into the castle and find out what had become of the goosey-gander. He quickly smuggled himself into the tin and concealed himself as well as he could under the anemones and colt's-foot.

He was barely hidden when the young man picked up the tin, hung it around his neck, and slammed down the cover.

Then the teacher came back, and said that they had been given permission to enter the castle. At first he conducted the students only as far as the courtyard, where he stopped and began to talk to them about this ancient structure.

He told them of how the first human beings who had inhabited this country, had been obliged to live in mountain-grottoes and earth-caves; in the dens of wild beasts, and in the brushwood; and that a very long period had elapsed before they learned to build themselves huts from the trunks of trees; and afterward, how long they had been forced to labour and struggle before they advanced from the log cabin, with its single room, to the building of a castle with a hundred rooms — like Vittskövle.

It was about three hundred and fifty years ago that the rich and powerful built such castles for themselves, he said. It was obvious that Vittskövle was erected at a time when wars and robbers made it unsafe in Skåne. All around the castle was a deep trench filled with water; and across this there had been a bridge in bygone days that could be hoisted. Over the gate-arch there was a watch-tower which stands there even to this day; and all along the sides of the castle ran sentry-galleries, and in the corners stood towers with walls a metre thick. Yet this castle was not erected in the most savage war times; for Jens Brahe, who built it, had taken pains to make of it a beautiful and decorative ornament. If they could see the big, solid stone structure at Glimminge, which was built only a generation earlier, they would readily see that Jens Holgersen Ulfstand, the builder, hadn't figured upon anything else than to build big and strong and secure — without bestowing a thought upon making it beautiful and comfortable. If they visited such castles as Marsvinsholm, Snogeholm, and

Ovid Cloister — which were erected a hundred years or so later—they would find that the times had become less warlike. The gentleman who built these places had not furnished them with fortifications; but had only taken care to provide themselves with great, splendid dwelling houses.

The teacher talked at length — and in detail; and the boy who lay shut up in the tin grew pretty impatient; but he must have lain very still, for the owner of the tin hadn't the least suspicion that he was carrying him along.

Finally the company went into the castle. But if the boy had hoped for a chance to crawl out of that tin he was mistaken; for the student carried it upon him all the while, and the boy was obliged to accompany him through all the rooms. It was a tedious tramp. The teacher stopped every other minute to explain and instruct.

In one room he found an old fireplace, and before this he stopped to talk about the different kinds of fireplaces that had been used in the course of time. The first indoors fireplace was a big, flat stone on the floor of the hut, with an opening in the roof which let in both wind and rain. The next was a big stone hearth with no opening in the roof. This must have made the hut very warm, but it also filled it with soot and smoke. When Vittskövle was built, the people had advanced far enough to open the fireplace, which, at that time, had a wide chimney for the smoke; but it also took most of the warmth up in the air with it.

If that boy had ever in his life been cross and impatient, he was given a good lesson in patience this day. It must have been a whole hour now that he had lain perfectly still.

In the next room they came to, the teacher paused before an old-time bed with its high canopy and rich curtains.

Immediately he began to talk about the beds and bed places of olden days.

The teacher didn't hurry himself; but then, he did not know, of course, that a poor little creature lay shut up in a botanist's tin only waiting for him to get through. When they came to a room with gilded leather hangings, he talked to them of how the people had dressed their walls and ceilings ever since the beginning of time. And when he came upon an old family portrait, he told them all about the different changes in dress. And in the banquet hall he described ancient customs of celebrating weddings and funerals.

Thereupon, the teacher talked a little about the excellent men and women who had lived in the castle: about the old Brahes, and the old Barnekows; of Christian Barnekow, who had given his horse to the king to help him escape; of Margareta Ascheberg who had been married to Kjell Barnekow and who, when a widow, had managed the estates and the whole district for fifty-three years; of banker Hagerman, a farmer's son from Vittskovle, who had grown so rich that he had bought the entire estate; of the Stjernsvärds, who had given the people of Skåne better ploughs, which enabled them to discard the ridiculous old wooden ploughs that three span of oxen were hardly able to drag. During all this, the boy lay still. If he had ever been mischievous and shut the cellar door on his father or mother, he understood now how they had felt; for it was hours and hours before that teacher got through.

At last the teacher went out into the courtyard again. And there he discoursed upon the tireless labour of mankind to procure for themselves tools and weapons, clothes and houses and ornaments. He said that an old castle like Vittskövle was a mile-post on time's highway. Here one could see how far the people had advanced three hundred and fifty years ago; and one could judge for one's self if things had gone forward or backward since their time.

But this dissertation the boy escaped hearing; for the student who carried him was thirsty again and stole into the kitchen to ask for a drink of water. Now that the boy had been brought to the kitchen, he should have tried to look around for the goosey-gander. He had begun to move; and in so doing he happened to press too hard against the lid — and it flew open. Botanists' tin-lids are always flying open so the student paid no special heed to this, but pressed it down again. Then the cook asked him if he had a snake in the box.

"No, I have only a few plants," the student replied. "It was certainly something that moved there," insisted the cook. The student threw back the lid to show her that she was mistaken. "See for yourself — if ——"

But he got no further, for now the boy dared not stay in the box any longer, but with a bound he was on the floor, and out he rushed. There was hardly time for the maids to see what it was that ran, but they hurried after it, nevertheless.

The teacher still stood and talked when he was interrupted by shrill cries. "Catch him, catch him!" shrieked those who had come from the kitchen; and all the young students, also, raced after the boy, who scurried away faster than a rat. They tried to intercept him at the gate, but it was not easy to get hold of such a little creature, so, luckily, he got out into the open.

The boy did not dare to run down toward the open avenue but turned in another direction. He rushed through the garden into the backyard. All the while the people raced after him, shrieking and laughing. The poor little thing ran as hard as ever he could to get out of their way; but still it looked as if the crowd would catch up with him.

As he was hurrying along past a labourer's cottage, he heard a goose cackle, and saw a white down lying on the doorstep. There, at last, was the goosey-gander! He had been on the wrong track before. He thought no more of housemaids and men who were hounding him, but climbed up the steps into the hallway. Farther he couldn't come, for the door was locked. He heard how the goosey-gander cried and moaned inside, but he couldn't get the door open. The hunters that were pursuing him came nearer and nearer, and, in the room, the goosey-gander cried more and more pitifully. In this direst of needs the boy finally plucked up courage and pounded on the door with all his might.

A child opened it, and the boy looked into the room. In the middle of the floor sat a woman who held the goosey-gander tight — to clip his quill-feathers. It was her children who had found him, and she didn't want to do him any harm. It was her intention to let him in among her own geese as soon as his wings were clipped, so he couldn't fly away. But a worse fate could hardly have happened to the goosey-gander, and he shrieked and moaned at the top of his voice.

And a lucky thing it was that the woman hadn't started the clipping sooner. Now only two quills had fallen under the shears when the door opened and the little pigmy stood on the threshold. But a creature like that the woman had never seen before. She couldn't believe but that it was Goa-Nisse himself; and in her terror she dropped the shears, clasped her hands — and forgot to hold on to the goosey-gander.

As soon as he felt himself freed, he ran toward the door. He didn't give himself time to stop; but, as he ran he grabbed the boy by the neckband and carried him along with him. On the stoop he spread his wings and rose up into the air; at the same time he made a graceful sweep with his neck and seated the boy on his smooth, downy back.

And off they flew — while all Vittskövle stood and stared after them.

IN ÖVID CLOISTER-PARK

ALL that day, while the wild geese played with the fox, the boy lay and slept in a deserted squirrel nest. When he awoke, toward evening, he felt very anxious. "Well, now I shall soon be sent home! Then, after all, I'll have to exhibit myself before father and mother," thought he. But when he looked up and saw the wild geese, who lay bathing in Vomb Lake, not one of them said a word about his going. "They probably think the white one is too tired to travel home with me to-night," thought the boy.

The next morning the geese were awake at daybreak, long before sunrise. Now the boy felt sure that he'd have to go home; but, curiously enough, both he and the white goosey-gander were permitted to follow the wild ones on their morning jaunt. The boy couldn't comprehend the reason of the delay, but he figured it out in this way, that the wild geese did not care to send the goosey-gander on such a long journey until both had eaten their fill. Come what might, he was only glad for every moment that should pass before he must face his parents.

The wild geese travelled over Ovid Cloister estate, which was situated in a beautiful park east of the lake, and which looked very imposing with its great castle; its well-planned court surrounded by low walls and pavilions; its fine old-time garden with covered arbours, streams, and fountains; its wonderful trees, trimmed bushes, and its evenly mown lawns with their beds of beautiful spring flowers.

As the wild geese flew over the estate in the early morning hour there was no human being about. When they had carefully assured themselves of this, they sank toward the dog kennel, and shouted: "What kind of a little hut is this? What kind of a little hut is this?"

Instantly the dog came out of his kennel — furiously angry — and barked at the air.

"Do you call this a hut, you tramps! Can't you see that this is a great stone castle? Can't you see what fine terraces, and what a lot of pretty walls and windows and great doors it has, bow, wow, wow, wow? Don't you see the grounds, can't you see the garden, can't you see the conservatories, can't you see the marble statues? You call this a hut, do you? Do huts have parks with beech-groves and hazel-bushes and trailing vines and oak trees and firs and hunting-grounds filled with game, wow, wow, wow? Do you call this a hut? Have you seen huts with so many outhouses around them that they look like a whole village? You must know of a lot of huts that have their own church and their own parsonage, and that rule over the district and the peasant homes and the neighbouring farms and barracks, wow, wow, wow? Do you call this a hut? To this *hut* belong the richest possessions in Skåne, you beggars! You can't see a bit of land, from where you hang in the clouds, that does not obey commands from this hut, wow, wow, wow!"

All this the dog managed to cry out in one breath; while the wild geese flew back and forth over the estate, and listened to him until he was winded. But then they cried: "What are you so mad about? We didn't ask about the castle; we only wanted to know about your kennel, stupid!"

When the boy heard this joke, he laughed; then a thought stole in on him which at once made him serious. "Think how many of these funny things you would hear, if only you could go with the wild geese through the whole country, all the way up to Lapland!" he said to himself. "And just now, when you are in such a bad fix, a trip like that would be the best thing you could hit upon."

The wild geese flew over to one of the wide fields, east of the estate, to eat grass-roots, and this they kept up for hours. In the meantime, the boy wandered in the great park which bordered the fields. He hunted up a beech-nut grove and began to look up at the bushes, to see if a nut from last fall still hung there. But again and again the thought of the trip came over him, as he walked in the park. He pictured to himself what a fine time he would have if he went with the wild geese. To freeze and starve: that he believed he should have to do often enough; but as a reward he would escape both work and study.

As he walked there, the old gray leader-goose came up to him and asked if he had found anything eatable. No, that he hadn't, he replied, and then she tried to help him. She couldn't find any nuts either, but she discovered a couple of dried blossoms that hung on a brier-bush. These the boy ate with a good relish. But he wondered what mother would say, if she knew that he had lived upon raw fish and old winter-dried blossoms.

When the wild geese had finally eaten all they could hold, they bore off toward the lake again, where they amused themselves with games until almost dinner time.

The wild geese challenged the white goosey-gander to take part in all kinds of sports. They had swimming races, running races, and flying races with him. The big tame one did his level best to hold his own, but the clever wild geese beat him every time. All the while, the boy sat on the goosey-gander's back and encouraged him, and he had as much fun as the rest. They laughed and screamed and cackled, and it was remarkable that the people on the estate did not hear them.

When the wild geese were tired of play, they flew out on the ice to rest a few hours. The afternoon they spent in much the same way as the forenoon. First, a couple of hours feeding, then bathing and play in the water, near the ice-edge, until sunset, when they immediately arranged themselves for sleep.

"This is just the life for me," thought the boy as he crept in under the gander's wing. "But by to-morrow, I suppose I'll be sent home."

Before he fell asleep, he lay thinking that if only he might go along with the wild geese he would escape all scoldings because he was lazy. Then he could cut loose every day, and his only worry would be to get something to eat. But he needed so little nowadays; and there would always be a way to get that.

So he pictured the whole scene to himself; what he would see, and all the adventures that he would be in on. Yes, it would be something different from the wear and tear at home. "If I could only go with the wild geese on their travels, I shouldn't grieve because I'd been transformed," thought the boy.

He wasn't afraid of anything — except being sent home; but not even on Wednesday did the geese say anything to him about going. That day passed in the same way as Tuesday; and the boy grew more and more contented with the outdoor life. He was thinking that here he had the lovely Ovid Cloister-Park, which was as large as a forest, all to himself; and he wasn't anxious to go back to the stuffy cabin and the little patch of ground there at home.

On Wednesday he firmly believed that the wild geese thought of keeping him; but on Thursday he lost hope again.

Thursday began just like the other days; the geese fed on the broad meadows, and the boy hunted for food in the park. After a while Akka came to him, and asked if he had found anything to eat. No, he had not; and then she looked up a dry caraway herb, which had kept all its tiny seeds intact.

When the boy had finished eating, Akka said that she thought he ran around in the park altogether too recklessly. She wondered if he knew how many enemies he had to guard against — he, who was so little. No, he didn't know anything at all about that. Then Akka began to enumerate them.

Whenever he walked in the park, she said that he must look out for the fox and the marten; when he came to the shores of the lake, he must think of the otters; when seated on the stone wall, he must not forget the weasels, who can crawl through the smallest holes; and if he wished to lie down and sleep on a pile of leaves, he must first find out if the adders were not sleeping their winter sleep in the same pile. As soon as he came out into the open fields, he was to keep an eye out for hawks and buzzards; for eagles and falcons that soar in the air. In the bramble-bush he could be captured by the sparrow-hawk; magpies and crows were to be found everywhere, and in these he mustn't place too much confidence. As soon as it was dusk, he must keep his ears open and listen for the big owls, who flew along with such soundless wing-strokes that they could come right upon him before he was aware of their presence.

When the boy heard that there were so many who were after his life, he comprehended that it would be well-nigh impossible for him to escape. He was not especially afraid to die, but he didn't like the idea of being eaten up, so he asked Akka what he should do to protect himself from carnivorous animals.

Akka answered at once that the boy should try to get on good terms with all the smaller animals in woods and fields: with the squirrel folk, and the hare family; with bullfinches and titmice and woodpeckers and larks. If he made friends with them, they could warn him against dangers, find hiding-places for him, and protect him.

But, later in the day, when the boy tried to profit by this counsel and turned to Sirle Squirrel to ask for his protection, it was plain that he did not care to help him. "You surely can't expect anything from me, or the rest of the small animals!" said Sirle. "Don't you think we know that you are Nils the goose boy, who tore down the swallow's nest last year, crushed the starling's eggs, threw baby crows in the marl-ditch, caught thrushes in snares, and put squirrels in cages? You just help yourself as best you can; and you may be thankful that we do not form a league against you, and drive you back to your own kind!"

This was just the sort of answer the boy would not have let go unpunished, in the days when he was Nils, the goose boy. But now he was only fearful lest the wild geese, too, had found out how wicked he could be. He had been so anxious lest he shouldn't be permitted to stay with the wild geese that he hadn't dared to get into the least little mischief since joining their company. It was true that he didn't have the power to do much harm now, but, little as he was, he could have destroyed many birds' nests and crushed many eggs, if he'd been a mind to. Now he had been good. He hadn't pulled a feather from a goose-wing, or given any one a rude answer; and every morning when calling upon Akka, he had always removed his cap, and bowed.

All day Thursday he kept thinking it was surely on account of his wickedness that the wild geese did not care to take him along up to Lapland. And that evening, when he heard that Sirle Squirrel's wife had been stolen, and her children were starving to death, he made up his mind to help them. We have already been told how well he succeeded.

When the boy came into the park on Friday, he heard the bullfinches sing in every bush, of how Sirle Squirrel's wife had been carried away from her children by cruel robbers, of how Nils, the goose boy, had risked his life among human beings in taking the little squirrel children to her.

"And who is so honoured in Övid Cloister-Park now, as Thumbietot!" sang the bullfinch; "he, whom all feared when he was Nils the goose boy. Sirle Squirrel will give him nuts; the poor hares are going to play with him; the small wild animals will carry him on their backs, and fly away with him when Smirre Fox approaches. The titmice are going to warn him against the hawk, and the finches and larks will sing of his valour."

The boy was absolutely certain that both Akka and the wild geese had heard all this. And yet, the whole Friday passed without one word said as to his remaining with them.

Up until Saturday the wild geese had fed in the fields around Övid, undisturbed by Smirre Fox.

But Saturday morning, when they came out into the meadow, he lay in wait for them, and chased them from one field to another, so that they were not allowed to eat in peace. When Akka understood that he didn't intend that they should be left in peace, she quickly came to a decision, rose into the air, and off she flew with her flock over Färs' plains and Linderöd's hills. They did not stop until they had arrived in the district of Vittskövle.

But at Vittskövle the goosey-gander was stolen, and how it happened has already been related. If the boy hadn't used all his wits to help him, he would never again have been found.

On Saturday evening, when the boy returned to Vomb Lake with the goosey-gander, he thought that he had done a good day's work, and wondered much what Akka and the wild geese would say to him. The wild geese were not at all sparing in their praises, but they did not speak the word he was longing to hear.

Then Sunday came around again. A whole week had gone by since the boy had become bewitched, and he was still just as little.

But he didn't appear to be giving himself any extra worry because of this. Sunday afternoon he sat huddled up in a big, fluffy osier-bush, down by the lake, and blew on a reed-pipe. All around him there sat as many finches and bullfinches and starlings as the bush could well hold — who sang songs which he tried to teach himself to play. But the boy was not at home in this art. He blew so false that the feathers raised themselves on all the little music-masters, who shrieked and fluttered in their despair. The boy laughed so heartily at their excitement that he dropped his pipe. He tried it again, and this time too it went just as badly. Then all the little birds wailed: "To-day you play worse than usual, Thumbietot? You don't take one true note! Where are your thoughts, Thumbietot?"

"They are elsewhere," said the boy — and that was true. He sat there and pondered how long he should be allowed to remain with the wild geese; or if he would be sent home perhaps to-day.

Finally the boy threw down his pipe and jumped from the bush. He had seen Akka and all the other wild geese coming toward him in a long row. They walked so uncommonly slow and dignified-like that the boy immediately understood that now he should learn what they intended to do with him.

When they finally paused Akka said: "You may well have reason to wonder at me, Thumbietot, who have not said thanks to you for saving me from Smirre Fox. But I am one of those who would rather give thanks in deeds than in words. I have sent word to the elf that bewitched you. At first he didn't want to hear anything about curing you; but I have sent message upon message to him, telling him how well you have conducted yourself among us. He greets you, and says that as soon as you turn back home you shall be human again."

But think of it! Just as happy as the boy had been when the wild goose began to speak, just that miserable was he when she had finished. He didn't say a word, but turned away and wept.

"What in all the world does this mean?" said Akka.

"It appears as though you were expecting more of me than I have offered you."

But the boy was thinking of the carefree days and the banter; of adventure and freedom and travel, high above the earth, that he should miss, and he actually bawled with grief. "I don't want to be human," said he. "I want to go with you to Lapland." "I'll tell you something," said Akka. "That elf is very touchy, and I'm afraid that if you do not accept his offer now, it will be difficult for you to coax him another time."

It was a strange thing about that boy — as long as he had lived, he had never cared for any one. He had not cared for his father or mother; not for the school teacher; not for his schoolmates; nor for the boys in the neighbourhood. All that they had wished to have him do — whether it had been work or play — he had only thought tiresome. Therefore there was no one whom he missed or longed for.

The only ones that he had come anywhere near agreeing with, were Osa, the goose girl, and little Mats — a couple of children who had tended geese in the fields, like himself. But he didn't care particularly for them either. No, far from it! "I don't want to be human," bawled the boy. "I want to go with you to Lapland. That's why I've been good for a whole week!" "I don't want to forbid you to come along with us as far as you like," said Akka, "but think first if you wouldn't rather go home again. A day may come when you will regret this."

"No," said the boy, "that's nothing to regret. I have never been so well off as here with you."

"Well then, let it be as you wish," said Akka.

"Thanks!" said the boy, and he felt so happy that he had to cry for very joy — just as he had cried before with sorrow.

"I DON'T WANT TO BE HUMAN," SAID HE

CHAPTER FOUR

GLIMMINGE CASTLE

BLACK RATS AND GRAY RATS

IN SOUTHEASTERN SKÅNE, not far from the sea, there is an old castle called Glimminge. It is a big substantial stone structure; and can be seen over the plain for miles around. It is not more than four stories high; but it is so ponderous that an ordinary farmhouse, which stands on the same estate, looks like a little children's playhouse by comparison.

The big stone house has such thick ceilings and walls that there is scarcely room in its interior for anything but the thick walls. The stairs are narrow, the entrances small, and the rooms few. That the walls might retain their strength, there are only the fewest number of windows in the upper stories, and none at all are to be found in the lower ones. In the old war times, the people were just as glad that they could shut themselves up in a strong and massive house like this as one is nowadays to be able to creep into furs in a snapping cold winter. But when the time of peace came, they did not care to live in the dark and cold stone halls of the old castle any longer. They have long since deserted the big Glimminge Castle, and moved into dwelling places where light and air can penetrate.

At the time that Nils Holgersson wandered around with the wild geese, there were no human beings in Glimminge

Castle; but for all that, it was not without inhabitants. Every summer there lived a stork couple in a large nest on the roof. In a nest in the attic lived a pair of gray owls, in the secret passages hung bats; in the kitchen oven lived an old cat; and down in the cellar there were hundreds of old black rats.

Rats are not held in very high esteem by other animals; but the black rats at Glimminge Castle were the exception. They were always mentioned with respect, because they had shown great valour in battle with their enemies, and great endurance under the terrible misfortunes which had befallen their kind. They nominally belonged to a rat folk that at one time had been very numerous and powerful but were now dying out. During a long period of time, the black rats owned Skåne and the whole country. They were to be found in every cellar; in every attic; in larders and cowhouses and barns; in breweries and flour-mills, in churches and castles; in every man-constructed building. But now they were banished from all this — and were almost extinct. Only in one and another old and secluded spot could one run across a few of them; and nowhere were they to be found in such large numbers as in Glimminge Castle.

When an animal folk die out, it is generally the human kind who are the cause of it; but such was not the case in this instance. The people had certainly struggled with the black rats, but they had not been able to do them any harm worth mentioning. Those who had conquered them were an animal folk of their own kind, called gray rats.

These gray rats had not lived in the land from time immemorial, like the black rats, but were descended from a couple of poor immigrants who had landed in Malmo from a Libyan sloop about a hundred years ago. They were homeless, starved-out wretches that stuck close to the harbour, swam in among the piles under the bridges, and ate refuse that had been thrown in the water. They never ventured into the city, which was owned by the black rats.

But gradually, as the gray rats increased in number, they grew bolder. At first they moved over to some waste places and condemned old houses which the black rats had abandoned. They hunted their food in gutters and dirt heaps, and made the most of all the rubbish which the black rats did not deign to take care of. They were hardy, contented and fearless; and within a few years they had become so powerful that they undertook to drive the black rats out of Malmö. They took from them attics, cellars, and storerooms, starved them out or bit them to death, for they were not at all afraid of fighting.

When Malmö was captured, they marched forward in small and large companies to conquer the whole country. It is almost impossible to comprehend why the black rats did not muster themselves into a great, united war-expedition to exterminate the gray rats, while these were still few in number. But the black rats were so certain of their power that they could not believe it possible for them to lose it. They sat still on their estates, and, in the meantime, the gray rats took from them farm after farm, city after city. They were starved out, forced out, rooted out. In Skåne they had not been able to maintain themselves in a single place except Glimminge Castle.

The old castle had such secure walls and such few rat passages led through these that the black rats had managed to protect themselves, and to prevent the gray rats from crowding in. Night after night, year after year, the struggle had continued between the aggressors and the defenders;

but the black rats had kept faithful watch, and had fought with the utmost contempt for death, and, thanks to the fine old house, they had always conquered.

It will have to be acknowledged that so long as the black rats were in power they were as much shunned by all other living creatures as the gray rats are in our day — and for just cause; they had thrown themselves upon poor, fettered prisoners, and tortured them; they had ravished the dead; they had stolen the last turnip from the cellars of the poor; bitten off the feet of sleeping geese; stolen eggs and chicks from the hens; and had committed a thousand depredations. But since they had come to grief, all this seemed to have been forgotten; and no one could help but marvel at the last of a race that had held out so long against its enemies.

The gray rats that lived in the courtyard at Glimminge and in the neighbourhood, kept up a continuous warfare and were always on the watch for every possible chance to capture the castle. One should think that they would have allowed the little company of black rats to occupy Glimminge Castle in peace, since they themselves had acquired all the rest of the country; but you may be sure this thought never occurred to them. They were wont to say that it was a point of honour with them to conquer the black rats at some time or other. But those who were acquainted with the gray rats must have known that it was because the human kind used Glimminge Castle as a storehouse for grain that the gray ones could not rest until they had gained possession of the place.

THE STORK

Monday, March twenty-eighth.

EARLY one morning the wild geese, who stood and slept on the ice in Vomb Lake, were awakened by long calls from the air. "Trirop, Trirop!" it sounded. "Trianut, the crane, sends greetings to Akka, the wild goose, and her flock. To-morrow will be the day of the great Crane Dance on Kullaberg."

Akka raised her head and answered at once: "Greetings and thanks! Greetings and thanks!"

With that, the cranes flew farther; and the wild geese heard them for a long time, while they travelled and called out over every field, and every wooded hill: "Trianut sends greetings. To-morrow will be the day of the great Crane Dance on Kullaberg."

The wild geese were very happy over this invitation. "You're in luck," they said to the white goosey-gander, "to be permitted to attend the great Crane Dance on Kullaberg!" "Is it then so remarkable to see cranes dance?" asked the goosey-gander. "It is something that you have never even dreamed about!" replied the wild geese.

"Now we must think out what we shall do with Thumbietot to-morrow, so that no harm will come to him while we run over to Kullaberg," said Akka. "Thumbietot shall not be left alone!" said the goosey-gander. "If the cranes won't let him see their dance, then I'll stay here with him."

"No human being has ever been permitted to attend the Animals' Congress, at Kullaberg," said Akka, "and I shouldn't dare to take Thumbietot along. But we'll discuss this more at length later in the day. Now we must first and foremost think about getting something to eat."

With that Akka gave the signal to adjourn. On this day she also sought her feeding-place a good distance away, on Smirre Fox's account, and she didn't alight until she came to the swampy meadows a little to the south of Glimminge Castle.

All that day the boy sat on the shores of a little pond, and blew on reed-pipes. He was out of sorts because he shouldn't see the Crane Dance, and he just couldn't say a word, either to the goosey-gander or to any of the others.

It was mighty hard that Akka should still doubt him. When a boy had given up being human, just to travel around with a few miserable wild geese, they surely ought to understand that he had no desire to betray them. Then, too, they ought to realize that when he had renounced so much to follow them, it was their duty to let him see all the wonders they could show him.

"I'll have to speak my mind right out to them," thought he. But hour after hour passed by still he hadn't come round to it. It may sound remarkable — but the boy had actually acquired a kind of respect for the old leader-goose. He felt that it was not easy to pit his will against hers.

On one side of the swampy meadow, where the wild geese fed, there was a broad stone hedge. Toward evening, when the boy finally raised his head to speak to Akka, his glance happened to rest on this hedge. He uttered a little cry of surprise, and instantly all the wild geese looked up, and stared in the same direction. At first, both the geese and the boy thought that all the round, gray stones in the hedge had acquired legs and had started on a run; but soon they saw that a company of rats was running there. They moved very rapidly, and ran forward packed tightly, line upon line, and they were so many that, for some time, they covered the entire stone hedge.

The boy had been afraid of rats, even when he was a big, strong human being. Then what must his feelings be now, when he was so tiny that two or three of them could overpower him! One shudder after another travelled down his spinal column as he stood and stared at them.

But strangely enough, the wild geese seemed to feel the same aversion toward the rats that he did. They did not speak to them; and when they were gone, they shook themselves as if their feathers had been mud-bespattered.

"So many gray rats abroad!" said Iksi from Vassijaure. "That's not a good omen."

The boy meant to take advantage of this opportunity to say to Akka that he thought she ought to let him go with them to Kullaberg, but he was prevented anew, for all of a sudden a big bird came down among the geese.

One could think, when looking at this bird, that he had borrowed body, neck, and head from a little white goose. But in addition, he had procured for himself large black wings, long red legs, and a thick bill, which was too large for the little head, and weighted it down until it gave him a sad and worried look.

Akka at once straightened out the folds of her wings, and courtesied many times as she approached the stork. She wasn't especially surprised to see him in Skåne so early in the spring, because she knew that the male storks always come over in good season to have a look at the nest, to make sure that it has suffered no damage during the winter, before the female storks go to the trouble of flying over the Baltic. But she very much wondered what could be the meaning of his seeking her out, since storks prefer to associate with members of their own family.

"I can hardly believe that there is anything amiss with your house, Herr Ermenrich," said Akka.

Now it was apparent that the old saying is true: A stork seldom opens his bill without complaining. But that which made the things he said sound all the more doleful was, that it was difficult for him to speak up. He stood a long time and only clattered with his bill; afterward he spoke in a hoarse and feeble voice. He complained about everything: the nest, which was situated at the very top of the roof-tree at Glimminge Castle, had been totally destroyed by winter storms; and no food could he get any more in Skåne. The people of Skåne were appropriating all his possessions. They dug out his marshes and laid waste his swamps. He intended to move away from this country, and never return to it again.

While the stork grumbled, Akka, the wild goose, who had neither home nor protection, could not help thinking to herself: "If I had things as comfortable as you have, Herr Ermenrich, I should be above complaining. You have remained a free and wild bird; and yet you stand so well with human beings that none will fire a shot at you, or steal an egg from your nest." But all this she kept to herself. To the stork she only remarked that she couldn't believe he would be willing to move from a house where storks had resided ever since it was built.

Then the stork suddenly asked the geese if they had seen the gray rats who were marching toward Glimminge Castle. When Akka replied that she had seen the horrid creatures, he began to tell her all about the brave black rats who, for years, had defended the castle. "But this night Glimminge Castle will fall into the gray rats' power," sighed the stork.

"And why just this night, Herr Ermenrich?" asked Akka.

"Well, because nearly all the black rats went over to Kullaberg last night," said the stork, "since they counted on all the rest of the animals also hurrying there. But you see that the gray rats have stayed at home; and now they are mustering to storm the castle to-night, when it will be defended by only a few old creatures who are too feeble to go over to Kullaberg. They'll probably accomplish their purpose. But I have lived there in harmony with the black rats so many years that the idea of living in a place inhabited by their enemies is not agreeable to me."

Akka understood now that the stork had become so enraged over the gray rats' mode of action that he had sought her out as an excuse to complain about them. But after the manner of storks, he had certainly done nothing to avert the disaster. "Have you sent word to the black rats, Herr Ermenrich?" she asked. "No," replied the stork, "that would be of no use. Before they can get back, the castle will be taken." "You mustn't be so sure of that, Herr Ermenrich," said Akka. "I know an old wild goose, I do, who would gladly prevent outrages of this kind."

When Akka said that, the stork raised his head and stared at her. And it was not surprising, for Akka had neither claws nor bill that were fit for fighting; and, in the bargain, she was a day bird, and as soon as it grew dark she fell helplessly asleep, while the rats did their fighting at night.

But Akka had evidently made up her mind to help the black rats. She called Iksi from Vassijaure, and ordered him to take the wild geese over to Vomb Lake; and when the geese made excuses, she said authoritatively: "I believe it will be best for us all that you obey me. I must fly over to the big stone house, and if you follow me, the people on the place will be sure to see us, and shoot us down. The only one that I want to take with me on this trip is

Thumbietot. He can be of great service to me because he has good eyes, and can keep awake at night."

The boy was in his most contrary mood that day. And when he heard what Akka said, he raised himself to his full height and stepped forward, his hands behind him and his nose in the air; for he intended to say that he most decidedly did not wish to take a hand in the fight with gray rats. She might look around for assistance elsewhere.

But the instant the boy was seen, the stork began to move. He had stood before, as storks generally stand, with head bent downward and the bill pressed against the neck. But now a gurgle was heard deep down in his windpipe, as though he would have laughed. Quick as a flash, he lowered his bill, grabbed the boy, and tossed him a couple of metres into the air. This feat he performed seven times, while the boy shrieked and the geese shouted: "What are you trying to do, Herr Ermenrich? That's not a frog. That's a human being, Herr Ermenrich."

Finally the stork put the boy down, entirely unhurt. Thereupon he said to Akka: "Now I'll fly back to Glimminge Castle, Mother Akka. All who live there were very much worried when I left. You may be sure they'll be very glad when I tell them that Akka, the wild goose, and Thumbietot, the human elf, are on their way to rescue them." With that the stork craned his neck, spread his wings, and darted off like an arrow when it leaves a well-drawn bow. Akka understood that he was making fun of her, but she didn't let it bother her. She waited until the boy had found his wooden shoes, which the stork had shaken off; then she put him on her back and followed the stork. On his own account, the boy made no objection, and said not a word about not wanting to go along. He had become so furious with the stork that he actually sat and puffed. That long, red-legged thing believed he was of no account just because he was little; but he would show him what kind of a man Nils Holgersson from West Vemmenhög was.

A couple of moments later Akka stood in the storks' nest at Glimminge Castle. It was a fine, large nest. It had a wheel as foundation, and over this lay several grass mats, and some twigs. The nest was so old that many shrubs and plants had taken root up there; and when the mother stork sat on her eggs in the round hole in the middle of the nest, she not only had the beautiful outlook over a goodly portion of Skåne to enjoy, but she had also the wild brier-blossoms and house-leeks to look upon.

Both Akka and the boy saw immediately that something was going on here, which turned up and down in the most regular order. At the edge of the stork-nest sat two gray owls, an old, gray-streaked cat, and a dozen old, decrepit rats with protruding teeth and watery eyes. They were not exactly the sort of animals one usually finds living peaceably together.

Not one among them turned to look at Akka, or to bid her welcome. They thought of nothing except to sit and stare at some long, gray lines, which hove into sight here and there — on the winter-naked meadows.

All the black rats were silent. It was plain that they were in deep despair, and probably knew that they could defend neither their own lives nor the castle. The two owls sat and rolled their big eyes, and twisted their great, encircling eyebrows, as they talked in hollow, ghost-like voices about the awful cruelty of the gray rats, and of how they would have to move away from their nest, since they had heard it said of them that they spared neither eggs nor baby birds. The old gray-streaked cat was sure that the gray rats would bite him to death, since they were coming into the castle in such great numbers, and he kept scolding the black rats all the while. "How could you be so idiotic as to let your best fighters go away?" said he. "How could you trust the gray rats? It is absolutely unpardonable!"

The twelve black rats did not say a word. But the stork, despite his misery, could not refrain from teasing the cat. "Don't worry so, Tommy House-cat!" said he. "Can't you see that Mother Akka and Thumbietot have come to save the castle? You may be certain that they'll succeed. Now I must stand up to sleep — and I do so with the utmost calm. To-morrow, when I awaken, there won't be a single gray rat left in Glimminge Castle."

The boy winked at Akka, and made a sign — as the stork stood at the very edge of the nest, with one leg drawn up for sleep — that he wanted to push him down to the ground; but Akka restrained him. She did not seem to be the least bit angry. Instead, she said in a confident tone of voice: "It would be pretty poor business if one who is as old as I am could not manage to get out of worse difficulties than this. If only Mr. and Mrs. Owl, who can stay awake all night, will fly off with a couple of messages for me, I think that all will go well."

Both owls were willing. Then Akka bade the gentleman owl go seek the black rats who had gone off, and counsel them to hurry home immediately. The lady owl he sent to Flammea, the steeple owl, who lived in Lund Cathedral, with a commission which was so secret that Akka dared confide it to her only in a whisper.

THE RAT CHARMER

It was drawing on toward midnight when the gray rats, after a diligent search, succeeded in finding an open air-hole which led to the cellar. This was rather high upon the wall; but the rats formed a rat-ladder and it wasn't long before the most daring among them sat in the air-hole, ready to force its way into Glimminge Castle outside whose walls so many of its forebears had fallen.

The gray rat sat still a moment in the hole, awaiting an attack from within. The commanders of the defenders was surely away, but she took for granted that the black rats who were still in the castle would not surrender without a struggle. With thumping heart, she listened for the slightest sound, but all was still. Then the leader of the gray rats plucked up courage and jumped down into the coal-black cellar.

One after another the gray rats followed the leader. They all kept very quiet; and all expected to be ambushed by the black rats. Not until so many of them had crowded into the cellar that the floor could hold no more, did they venture farther.

Although they had never before been inside the building, they had no difficulty in finding their way. They soon found the passages in the walls which the black rats had used to get to the upper floors. Before they began to clamber up these narrow and steep steps, they listened again with great attention. They felt more frightened at the black rats holding themselves aloof in this way than if they had met them in open battle. They could hardly believe their luck when they had reached the first story without mishaps.

Immediately upon their entrance the gray rats scented the grain, which was stored in great bins on the floor. But it was not yet time for them to enjoy their conquest. They searched first, with the utmost caution, through the sombre, empty rooms. They ran up into the fireplace, which stood on the floor in the old castle kitchen, and they almost tumbled into the well, in the inner room. Not one of the narrow peep-holes did they leave uninspected, but they found no black rats. When this floor was wholly in their possession, they began, with the same caution, to acquire the next. Then they had to venture on a bold and dangerous climb through the walls, while, with breathless anxiety, they awaited an assault from the enemy. And although they were tempted by the most delicious odour from the grain bins, they forced themselves most systematically to inspect the old-time warriors' pillar-propped kitchen; their stone table and fireplace; the deep window-niches, and the hole in the floor — which in olden times had been opened to pour down boiling pitch on the intruding enemy.

All this time the black rats were invisible. The gray ones groped their way to the third story, and into the lord of the castle's great banquet hall, which stood there cold and empty like all the other rooms in the old house. They even groped their way to the upper story, which had but one big, barren room. The only place they did not think of exploring was the big stork-nest on the roof — where, just at this time, the lady owl awakened Akka, and informed her that Flammea, the steeple owl, had granted her request, and had sent her the thing she wished for.

Since the gray rats had so conscientiously inspected the entire castle, they felt at ease. They took for granted that the black rats had fled, and that they would offer no resistance. So with light hearts, they ran up into the grain bins.

But the gray rats had hardly swallowed the first wheat-grains, when the sound of a little shrill pipe was heard from the courtyard. The gray rats raised their heads, listened anxiously, ran a few steps, as if to leave the bin, then they turned back and began to eat once more.

Again the pipe sounded a sharp and piercing note — and now something wonderful happened. One rat, two rats — yes, a whole lot of rats left the grain, jumped from the bins and hurried down cellar by the shortest cut, to get out of the house. Still there were many gray rats left. These thought of all the toil and trouble it had cost them to win Glimminge Castle, and they did not want to leave it. But again they caught the tones from the pipe, and had to follow them. Wildly excited, they rushed up from the bins, slid down through the narrow holes in the walls, tumbling over each other in their eagerness to get out.

In the middle of the courtyard stood a tiny creature, who blew upon a pipe. All around him was a whole circle of rats who listened to him astonished and fascinated; and each moment brought more. Once he took the pipe from his lips — only for a second — put his thumb to his nose and wiggled his fingers at the gray rats; and then it looked as if they were ready to throw themselves on him and bite him to death; but as soon as he blew on his pipe they were in his power.

When the tiny creature had played all the gray rats out of Glimminge Castle, he began to wander slowly from the courtyard out into the highway; and all the gray rats followed him, because the tones from that pipe sounded so sweet to their ears that they could not resist them.

The tiny creature walked before them and charmed them along on the road to Vallby. He led them into all sorts of crooks and turns and bends — on through hedges and down into ditches — and wherever he went, they had to follow. He blew continuously on his pipe, which appeared to be made from an animal's horn, although the horn was so small that there were no animals in our day from whose foreheads it could have been broken. Nor did any one know who had made it. Flammea, the steeple owl, had found it in a niche, in Lund Cathedral. She had shown it to Bataki, the raven; and the two of them had figured out that this was the kind of horn that was used in former times by those who wished to gain power over rats and mice. But the raven was Akka's friend; and it was from him she had learned that Flammea owned such a treasure.

And it was true that the rats could not resist the pipe. The boy walked before them and played as long as the starlight lasted — and all the while they followed him. He played at daybreak; he played at sunrise; and the whole time the entire procession of gray rats followed him, and were enticed farther and father away from the big grain loft at Glimminge Castle.

CHAPTER FIVE

THE GREAT CRANE DANCE ON KULLABERG

Tuesday, March twenty-ninth.

ALTHOUGH there are many magnificent structures in Skåne, it must be granted that not one among them has such pretty walls as old Kullaberg.

Kullaberg is low and rather long. It is by no means a big or imposing mountain. On its broad summit you'll find woods and grain fields, and one and another heather-heath. Here and there, round heather-knolls and barren cliffs rise up. It is not especially pretty up there. It looks very much like all the other upland places in Skåne.

He who walks along the road which runs across the middle of the mountain can't help but feel a little disappointed. Then mayhap he turns from the path, wanders off toward the mountain's sides and looks down over the bluffs; and then, all at once, he discovers so much that is worth seeing he hardly knows how he'll find time to take in the whole of it. For it happens that Kullaberg does not stand on the land, with plains and valleys around it, like other mountains; but it has plunged into the sea, as far out as it can get. Not even the tiniest strip of land lies below the mountain to protect it against the breakers; for these reach all the way up to the mountain walls, and can polish and mould them to suit themselves. This is why the walls stand there as richly ornamented as the sea and its helpmeet, the wind, have been able to effect.

You'll find steep ravines deeply chiselled in the mountain's sides; and black crags that have become smooth and shiny under the constant lashing of the winds. There are solitary rock-columns that spring straight up out of the water, and dark grottoes with narrow entrances; there are barren, perpendicular precipices, and soft, leaf-clad inclines; there are small points, and small inlets, and small rolling stones that are rattlingly washed up and down with every dashing breaker; there are majestic cliff-arches which project over the water; there are sharp stones that are constantly being sprayed by a white foam; and others that mirror themselves in unchangeable dark-green still water. There are also giant troll-caverns shaped in the rock, and great crevices that tempt the wanderer to venture into the mountain's depths, all the way to Kullman's Hollow.

And over and around all these rocky steeps creep entangled tendrils and weeds. Trees grow there also, but the wind's power is so great that the trees have to transform themselves into clinging vines, that they may get a firmer hold on the steep precipices. The oaks creep along on the ground, while their foliage hangs over them like a low ceiling; and long-limbed beeches stand in the ravines like great leafy tents.

These remarkable mountain walls, with the blue sea beneath them and the clear penetrating air above them, are what make Kullaberg so dear to the people that great crowds haunt the place every day as long as the summer lasts. But it is more difficult to tell what it is that makes the place so attractive to animals that every year they gather there for a big play-meeting. This is a custom which has been observed from time immemorial; and one should have been there when the first sea-wave was dashed into foam against the shore, to be able to explain why just Kullaberg was chosen as a meeting ground in preference to all other places.

When the meeting is to take place, the stags and roebucks and hares and foxes and all the other four-footers make the journey to Kullaberg the night before, so as not to be observed by the human kind. Just before sunrise they all march up to the playground, which is a heather-heath on the left side of the road, and not very far from the mountain's outermost point. The playground is inclosed on all sides by round knolls, which conceal it from any and all who do not happen to come right upon it. And in the month of March it is not at all likely that any pedestrian will stray off up there. All strangers who at other times stroll around on the rocks and clamber up the mountain side, the fall storms have driven away these many months. The lighthouse keeper out there, on the point; the old *fru* on the mountain farm, and the mountain peasant and his house folk go their accustomed ways, and do not run about on the desolate heaths.

When the four-footers have arrived on the playground, they take their places on the round knolls. Each animal family keeps to itself, although it is understood that on a day like this universal peace reigns, and none need fear attack. On this day a little hare might wander over to the foxes' hill, without losing so much as one of its long ears. All the same the animals arrange themselves into separate groups. This is an old custom.

After all have taken their places, they begin to look around for the birds. It is always beautiful weather on this day. The cranes are good weather prophets, and would not call the animals together if rain was expected.

Although the air is clear and nothing obstructs the vision, the four-footers see no birds. This is strange. The sun is high in the heavens, and the birds should already be on their way.

However, what the animals do observe is one and another little dark cloud slowly advancing over the plain. And look! one of these clouds comes suddenly along the coast of Öresund, and up toward Kullaberg. When the cloud has come just above the playground it stops, and all of a sudden the entire cloud begins to ring and chirp, as if it were made up of nothing but tone. It rises and sinks, rises and sinks, but all the while it rings and chirps. At last the whole cloud falls down over a knoll — all at once — the next instant the knoll is entirely covered with gray larks, pretty red-gray-white bullfinches, speckled starlings and greenish-yellow titmice.

Soon after that, another cloud comes over the plain. This stops over every bit of land: over peasant cottage and palace; over towns and cities; over farms and railway stations; over fishing hamlets and sugar refineries. Every time it stops, it draws to itself a little whirling column of gray dust-grains from the ground. Thus it grows and grows. And at last, when it is all gathered up and heads for Kullaberg, it is no more a cloud but a whole mist which is so big that it throws a shadow on the ground all the way from Höganäs to Mölle. When it stops over the playground it hides the sun; and for a long while it had to rain gray sparrows on one of the knolls before those who had been flying in the innermost part of the mist could again catch a glimpse of the daylight.

But still the biggest of these bird-clouds is the one which now appears. This is formed of birds who have travelled from every direction to join it. It is dark bluish-gray, and no sun-ray can penetrate it. And it is full of the ghastliest noises, the most frightful shrieks, the grimmest laughter, and most ill-luck-boding croaking! All on the playground are glad when it finally resolves itself into a storm of fluttering and croaking: of crows and jackdaws and rooks and ravens.

Thereupon not only clouds are seen in the heavens, but also a variety of stripes and figures. Then straight, dotted lines appear in the East and Northeast. These are forest-birds from the Göinge districts: black grouse and wood grouse come flying in long lines a couple of metres apart. Swimming-birds that live around Måkläppen, just out of Falsterbo, now come floating over Oresund in many extraordinary figures: in triangular and long curves; in sharp hooks and semicircles.

To the great reunion held the year that Nils Holgersson travelled around with the wild geese, came Akka and her flock — later than all the others. And that was not to be wondered at, for Akka had to fly over the whole of Skåne to get to Kullaberg. Besides, as soon as she awoke, she was obliged to go out and hunt for Thumbietot, who, for many hours, had gone and played to the gray rats, and lured them far away from Glimminge Castle. Mr. Owl had returned with the news that the black rats would be at home immediately after sunrise; and now it was quite safe to let the steeple owl's pipe be hushed, and to give the gray rats the liberty of going where they pleased.

It was not Akka who discovered the boy, where he walked with his long following, and quickly sank down over him and caught him up with the bill and swung into the air; but Herr Ermenrich, the stork! For Herr Ermenrich had also gone out to look for him. And after he had borne him up to the stork-nest, he begged his forgiveness for having treated him with disrespect the evening before.

This pleased the boy immensely, and the stork and he became good friends. Akka, too, showed that she felt very kindly toward him; she stroked her old head several times against his arms, and commended him because he had helped those who were in trouble.

But this much must be said to the boy's credit: he did not want to accept praise which he had not earned. "No, Mother Akka," he said, "you mustn't think that I lured the gray rats away to help the black ones. I only wanted to show Herr Ermenrich that I was of some consequence."

No sooner had he said this than Akka turned to the stork and asked if he thought it advisable to take Thumbietot along to Kullaberg. "I mean, that we can rely on him as upon ourselves," said she. The stork at once insisted most enthusiastically that Thumbietot be permitted to come along. "Of course you shall take Thumbietot along to Kullaberg, Mother Akka," said he. "It is our good fortune that we can repay him for all that he has endured this night for our sakes. And since it still grieves me to think that I did not conduct myself in a becoming manner toward him the other evening, it is I who will carry him on my back — all the way to the meeting place.'

There isn't much that tastes better than praise from those who are wise and capable; and the boy had certainly never felt so happy as when the wild goose and the stork talked about him in this way.

Thus the boy made the trip to Kullaberg, riding storkback. Although he knew that this was a great honour, it caused him much anxiety, for Herr Ermenrich was a master flyer, and started off at a pace very different from that of the wild geese. While Akka flew her straight way with even wing-strokes, the stork amused himself by performing a lot of flying tricks. First he lay still in an immeasurable height, and floated in the air without moving his wings, then he flung himself downward with such sudden haste that it seemed as if he would fall to the ground, helpless as a stone; and then he had heaps of fun flying all around Akka, in great and small circles, like a whirlwind. The boy had never before been on a ride of this sort; and though he sat there all the while in terror, he had to admit to himself that never before had he known what a good flight meant.

Only a single pause was made during the journey, and that was at Vomb Lake, where Akka joined her travelling companions and called out to them that the gray rats had been vanquished. After that, the travellers flew straight on to Kullaberg.

There they descended to the knoll reserved for the wild geese; and as the boy let his glance wander from knoll to knoll, he noticed on one the many-pointed antlers of the stags; and on another, the gray herons' neck-crests. One knoll was red with foxes, one was gray with rats; one was covered with black ravens who shrieked continually; and one with larks who simply couldn't keep still, but kept bounding into the air and singing for very joy

As has ever been the custom on Kullaberg, it was the crows that began the day's games and frolics with their flying dance. They divided themselves into two flocks, that flew toward each other, met, turned, and then began all over again. This dance had many repetitions, and appeared to the spectators who were not familiar with the dance as altogether too monotonous. The crows were very proud of their dance, but all the others were glad when it was over. It appeared to the animals to be about as gloomy and meaningless as the winter storms' play with the snowflakes. It depressed them to watch it, and they waited eagerly for something that should give them a little pleasure.

Nor did they not have to wait in vain. For as soon as the crows had finished, the hares came running. They dashed forward in a long row, with no marked order. In some of the figures came one single hare; in others, they ran three and four abreast. All had risen on two legs, and were rushing forward with such rapidity that their long ears flapped in all directions. As they ran, they spun round, made high leaps, and beat their fore-paws against their hind-paws so that they rattled. Some performed a long succession of somersaults, others doubled themselves up and rolled over like wheels; one stood on one leg and swung round; one walked on his fore-paws. There was no regulation whatever, yet there was much that was droll in the hares' play; and the many animals who looked on began to breathe faster. Now it was spring; joy and rapture were advancing. Winter was over; summer was coming. Soon it was only play to live.

When the hares had romped themselves out, it was the great forest birds' turn to perform. Hundreds of wood grouse in shining dark-brown array, and with bright red eyebrows, shot up into a great oak that stood in the centre of the playground. The one who sat upon the topmost branch fluffed up his feathers, lowered his wings, and lifted his tail so that the white covert-feathers were seen. Thereupon he stretched his neck and sent forth a couple of deep notes from his thick throat. "Tjack, tjack, tjack," it sounded. More than this he could not utter. There were only a few gurgles way down in the throat. Then he closed his eyes and whispered: "Sis, sis, sis. Hear how pretty! Sis, sis, sis." At the same time he fell into such an ecstasy that he no longer knew what was going on around him.

While the first wood grouse was sissing, the three nearest — under him — began to sing; and before they had finished their song, the ten who sat lower down, joined in; and thus it continued from branch to branch, until the entire hundred grouse sang and gurgled and sissed. They all fell into the same ecstasy during their song, and this affected the other animals like a contagious transport. Lately the blood had flowed lightly and agreeably; now it began to grow heavy and hot. "Yes, this is surely spring," thought all the animal folk. "Winter chill has vanished. The fires of spring burn over the earth."

When the black grouse saw that the brown grouse were having such success, they could no longer keep quiet. As there was no tree for them to light upon, they rushed down to the playground, where the heather stood so high that only their beautifully turned tail-feathers and their thick bills were visible — and they began to sing: "Orr, orr, orr."

Just as the black grouse started to compete with the brown grouse, something unprecedented happened. While all the animals were thinking of nothing but the grouse-game, a fox stole slowly over to the wild geese's knoll. He glided very cautiously, and was far up on the knoll before any one noticed him. Suddenly a goose caught sight of him; and as she could not believe that a fox had sneaked in among the geese for any good purpose, she began to cry: "Have a care, wild geese! Have a care!" The fox struck her across the throat — mostly, perhaps, because he wanted to make her keep quiet — but the wild geese had already heard the cry, so they all rose into the air. When they had flown, the animals saw Smirre Fox standing on the wild geese's knoll, with a dead goose in his mouth.

But because he had thus broken the play-day's peace, such a punishment was meted out to Smirre Fox, that for the rest of his days he must regret that he had not been able to control his thirst for revenge, but had attempted to approach Akka and her flock in this manner.

He was immediately surrounded by a crowd of foxes and doomed in accordance with an old custom, which demands that whosoever disturbs the peace on the great play-day must go into exile. Not a fox wished to lighten the sentence, since they all knew that the instant they attempted anything of the sort, they would be driven from the playground, and would nevermore be permitted to enter it. Banishment was pronounced upon Smirre without opposition. He was forbidden to remain in Skåne. He was banished from wife and kindred; from hunting grounds, home, resting places, and retreats, which he had hitherto owned; and he must tempt fortune in foreign lands. So that all foxes in Skåne should know that Smirre was outlawed in the district, the oldest of the foxes bit off his right earlap. As soon as this was done, all the young foxes began to yowl with blood-thirst, throwing themselves on Smirre. For him there was no way out but to take to his feet; and with all the young foxes in hot pursuit, he rushed from Kullaberg.

All this happened while black grouse and brown grouse were going on with their games. But these birds lose themselves so completely in their song that they neither hear nor see. Nor had they permitted themselves to be disturbed.

The forest birds' contest was barely over, when the stags from Häckeberga came forward to show their wrestling game. There were several pairs of stags who fought at the same time. They rushed at each other with tremendous force, struck their antlers clashingly together, so that their points were entangled, trying to force each other backward. The heather-heaths were torn up beneath their hoofs; the breath came like smoke from their nostrils; out of their throats strained hideous bellowings, and the froth oozed down on their flanks.

On the knolls round about there was breathless silence while the skilled stag-wrestlers clinched. In all the animals new emotions were awakened. Each and all felt courageous and strong; enlivened by returning powers; born again with the spring; sprightly, and ready for all kinds of adventures. They felt no enmity toward each other, although, everywhere, wings were lifted, neck-feathers raised, and claws sharpened. If the stags from Häckeberga had continued another instant, a wild struggle would have arisen on the knolls, for all had been gripped with a burning desire to show that they, too, were full of life because the winter's impotence was over and strength surged through their bodies.

But the stags stopped wrestling just at the right moment, and instantly a whisper went from knoll to knoll: "The cranes are coming!"

And then came the gray, dusk-clad birds with plumes in their wings, and red feather-ornaments on their necks. The big birds with their tall legs, their slender throats, their small heads, came gliding down the knoll with an abandon that was full of mystery. As they glided forward they swung round — half flying, half dancing. With wings gracefully lifted, they moved with an inconceivable rapidity. There was something marvellous and strange about their dance. It was as though gray shadows had played a game which the eye could scarcely follow. It was as if they had learned it from the mists that hover over desolate swamps. There was witchcraft in it. All those who had never before been on Kullaberg understood now why the whole meeting took its name from the cranes' dance. There was wildness in it; but yet the feeling which it awakened was a delicious longing. No one thought any more about struggling. Instead, both the winged and those who had no wings, all wanted to raise themselves eternally, lift themselves above the clouds, seek that which was hidden beyond them, leave the oppressive body that dragged them down to earth and soar away toward the infinite.

Such longing after the unattainable, after the hidden mysteries back of this life, the animals felt only once a year; and this was on the day when they beheld the Great Crane Dance.

CHAPTER SIX

IN RAINY WEATHER

Wednesday, March thirtieth.

IT WAS the first rainy day of the trip. So long as the wild geese had remained in the vicinity of Vomb Lake they had had beautiful weather; but on the day they set out to travel farther north, it began to rain, and for several hours the boy had to sit on the goose-back, soaking wet, and shivering with the cold.

In the morning, when they had started, it was clear and mild. The wild geese had flown high up in the air, steadily, and without haste — with Akka at the head maintaining strict discipline, and the rest in two oblique lines behind her. They had not taken time to shout any cutting remarks to the animals on the ground; but, as it was simply impossible for them to keep perfectly silent, they sang out continually in rhythm with the wing-strokes their usual coaxing call: "Where are you? Here am I. Where are you? Here am I."

All took part in this persistent calling, only stopping, now and then, long enough to show the goosey-gander the landmarks they were travelling over.

It was a monotonous trip, and when the rain-clouds made their appearance the boy thought it a real diversion. In the old days, when he had seen rain-clouds only from below, he had thought them gray and disagreeable; but it was a very different thing to be up amongst them. Now he saw distinctly that the clouds were enormous carts, which drove through the heavens with sky-high loads. Some were piled up with huge, gray sacks, some with barrels; others were so large that they could hold a whole lake; and a few were filled with big utensils and bottles which were piled up to an immense height. And when so many of them had driven forward that they filled the whole sky, it appeared as if some one had given a signal, for all at once, water began to pour down over the earth, from utensils, barrels, bottles, and sacks.

Just as the first spring showers pattered against the ground there arose such shouts of joy from all the small birds in groves and pastures that the whole air rang with them, and the boy leaped high where he sat. "Now we'll have rain. Rain gives us spring; spring gives us flowers and green leaves; green leaves and flowers give us worms and insects; worms and insects give us food; and plentiful, and good food is the best thing there is," sang the birds.

The wild geese, too, were glad of the rain which came to awaken the growing things from their long sleep, and to drive holes in the ice-roofs on the lakes. They were not able to keep up that seriousness any longer, but began to send merry calls over the neighbourhood.

When they flew over the big potato patches, which are so plentiful in the country around Christianstad and which still lay bare and black — they screamed: "Wake up and be useful! Here comes something that will awaken you. You have idled long enough now."

When they saw people running to get out of the rain, they reproved them saying: "What are you in such a hurry about? Can't you see that it's raining rye-loaves and cookies?"

A big, thick mist was moving swiftly northward following close upon the geese. They seemed to think that they were dragging the mist along with them; and, just now, when they saw great orchards beneath them, they called out proudly: "Here we come with crocuses; here we come with roses; here we come with apple blossoms and cherry buds; here we come with peas and beans and turnips and cabbages. He who wills can take them. He who wills can take them."

Thus it had sounded while the first showers fell, and when all were still glad of the rain. But when the rain continued to fall the whole afternoon, the wild geese grew impatient, and cried to the thirsty forests around Ivo Lake: "Haven't you got enough yet? Haven't you got enough yet?"

The heavens were growing grayer and grayer and the sun hid itself so well that one couldn't imagine where it was. The rain fell faster and faster, and beat harder and harder against the wings, as it tried to find its way between the oily outside feathers, into their skins. The earth was hidden by fogs; lakes, mountains, and woods floated together in an indistinct maze, and the landmarks could not be distinguished. The flight became slower and slower; the joyful cries were hushed; and the boy felt the cold more and more keenly.

But he had kept up his courage as long as he had ridden through the air. And in the afternoon, when they had alighted under a little stunted pine in the middle of a large swamp, where all was wet, and all was cold; where some knolls were covered with snow, and others stood up naked in a puddle of half-melted ice-water, even then, he had not felt discouraged, but had run about in fine spirits, hunting for cranberries and frozen whortle-berries. But then came the evening, and darkness sank down on them so close that not even such eyes as the boy's could see through it; and all the wilderness became so strangely grim and awful. The boy lay tucked in under the goosey-gander's wing, but could not sleep because he was cold and wet. He heard such a lot of rustling and rattling and stealthy steps and menacing voices, that he became terror-stricken and didn't know where he should go. He must go somewhere where there was light and heat, if he didn't want to die of fright.

"Suppose I venture where there are human beings, just for this one night——" thought the boy, "only to sit by a fire for a moment, and to get a little food. I could get back to the wild geese before sunrise."

He crept from under the wing and slid down to the ground. He didn't awaken the goosey-gander or any of the other geese, but stole silently and unobserved, through the swamp.

He didn't know exactly where on earth he was: if he was in Skåne, in Småland, or in Blekinge. But just before reaching the swamp he had glimpsed a large village, and thither he directed his steps. Nor was it long before he discovered a road. Soon he was in the village street, which was long, and had trees on both sides, and was bordered with garden after garden.

The boy had come to one of the big cathedral towns, which are so common on the uplands, but which can hardly be seen at all down on the plain.

The houses were of wood, and very prettily constructed. Most of them had gables and fronts, edged with carved mouldings, and glass doors—with here and there a coloured pane — opening on verandas. The walls were painted in light colours; the doors and window-frames shone in blues and greens, and even in reds. While the boy walked about and viewed the houses, he could hear, all the way out to the road, how the people who sat in the warm cottages chattered and laughed. He could not distinguish their words but all the same he thought it was just lovely to hear human voices. "I wonder what they would say if I knocked and begged to be let in," thought he.

This of course had been his intention all along, but now that he saw the lighted windows his fear of the darkness was gone. Instead, he felt again that sense of shyness which always came over him now when he was near human beings. "I'll try to see a little more of the town," thought he, "before I ask any one to take me in."

One house he came to had a balcony. And just as the boy walked by, the doors were thrown open, and a yellow light streamed through the fine, sheer curtains. Then a pretty young lady came out upon the balcony and leaned over the railing. "It's raining; now we shall soon have spring," said she. When the boy saw her he felt a strange longing. It was as though he wanted to weep. For the first time he was a bit sorry that he had shut himself out from the human kind.

Shortly after, he came to a shop outside of which stood a red corn-drill. He stopped and looked at it, and finally crawled upto the seat, and made believe he was driving. He was thinking what fun it would be to drive such a pretty machine over a grainfield. For the moment he had forgotten what he was like now; then he remembered, and quickly jumped down from the machine. Then an even greater unrest came over him. After all human beings were very wonderful and clever!

As he walked by the post-office, he thought of all the

newspapers that came every day with news from the four corners of the earth. He saw the apothecary's shop and the doctor's home, and marvelled at the power of human beings, who could battle against sickness and death. He came to the church. Then he thought of how human beings had built it, that they might hear about another world than the one in which they lived; of God and the resurrection and eternal life. And the longer he walked there, the better he liked human beings.

It is thus with children: they never think any further ahead than the length of their tiny noses. That which lies nearest them they want promptly, with never a thought as to what it may cost them. Nils Holgersson had not understood what he was losing when he chose to remain an elf; but now he began to be dreadfully afraid that perhaps he should never again get back his right form.

How in all the world should he go to work in order to become human? This he wanted, oh! so much, to know.

He crawled upon a doorstep, seated himself in the pouring rain, and meditated. He sat there one whole hour — two whole hours, and he thought so hard that his forehead lay in furrows; but he was none the wiser. It seemed as if the thoughts only rolled round and round in his head. The longer he sat there, the more impossible it seemed to him to find any solution.

"This thing is certainly much too difficult for one who has learned so little as I have," he thought at last. "It will probably end in my having to go back among human beings after all. I must ask the minister and the doctor and the schoolmaster and others who are learned, and may know of a cure for such things."

This he determined to do at once, and shook himself —for he was as wet as a dog that has been in a pool.

Just then he saw a big owl come flying! It lit in one of the trees that bordered the village street. The next instant a lady owl, who sat under a cornice of the house, began to call out: "Kivitt, Kivitt! Are you at home again, Mr. Gray Owl? What kind of a time did you have abroad?"

"Thank you, Lady Brown Owl, I had a delightful time," said the gray owl. "Has anything out of the ordinary happened here at home during my absence?"

"Not here in Blekinge, Mr. Gray Owl; but in Skåne a marvellous thing has happened! A boy has been transformed by an elf into a goblin no bigger than a squirrel; and since then he has gone to Lapland with a tame goose."

"That's a remarkable bit of news, a remarkable bit of news. Can he never be human again, Lady Brown Owl? Can he never be human again?"

"That's a secret, Mr. Gray Owl; but you shall hear it just the same. The elf has said that if the boy watches over the goosey-gander, so that he comes home safe and sound, and ——"

"What more, Lady Brown Owl? What more? What more?"

"Fly with me up to the church tower, Mr. Gray Owl, and you shall hear the whole story! I fear there may be some one listening down here in the street." With that, the owls flew their way; but the boy flung his cap in the air, and shouted: "If I only watch over the goosey-gander, so that he gets back safe and sound, then I shall become a human being again. Hurrah! Hurrah! Then I shall become a human being again!"

He shouted "hurrah" until it was strange that they did not hear him in the houses — but they didn't, and he hurried back to the wild geese, out in the wet morass, as fast as his legs could carry him.

Chapter Seven

THE STAIRWAY WITH THE THREE STEPS

Thursday, March thirty-first.

THE following day the wild geese were to travel northward through Allbo district, in Småland. They sent Iksi and Kaksi to spy out the land. But when they returned, they said that all the water was frozen, and all the land was snow-covered. "We may as well remain where we are," said the wild geese. "We cannot travel over a country where there is neither water nor food."

"If we remain where we are, we may have to wait here until the next moon," said Akka. "It is better to go eastward, through Blekinge, and see if we can't get to Småland by way of Möre, which is near the coast, and has an early spring."

Thus the boy came to ride over Blekinge that day. Now that it was light again, he was in a merry mood once more, and couldn't imagine what had come over him the night before. He certainly didn't want to give up the journey and the outdoor life now.

There was a thick fog over Blekinge, so the boy couldn't see how it looked out there. "I wonder if it is a rich or a poor land that I'm riding over," thought he, and tried to search his memory for the things he had heard about the country at school. But at the same time he knew well enough that this was useless, since he had never been in the habit of studying his lessons.

Suddenly the boy seemed to see the school before him — the children sitting at their little desks with raised hands; the teacher on the lectern looking displeased, and he himself before the map to answer some question about Blekinge; but he hadn't a word to say. The schoolmaster's face grew darker and darker for every second that passed, and the boy thought the teacher was more particular that they should know their geography than anything else. Now he came down from the lectern, took the pointer from the boy, and sent him back to his seat. "This won't end well," the boy had thought then.

But the schoolmaster had gone over to a window, and had stood there a moment looking out, and then he whistled to himself. He went back to the lectern saying that he would tell them something about Blekinge. And that which he then told was so amusing that the boy had listened. Now as he stopped to think for a moment, he remembered every word.

"Småland is a tall house with spruce trees on the roof," said the teacher, "and leading up to it is a broad stairway with three big steps; this stairway is called Blekinge. It is a stairway that is well constructed, and stretches forty-two miles along the frontage of Småland house, and any one who wishes to go all the way down to the Baltic Sea by way of the stairs, has twenty-four miles to climb.

"A good long time must have elapsed since the stairway was built. Both days and years have passed since the steps were hewn from gray stones and laid down evenly and smoothly, for a convenient track between Småland and the Baltic Sea.

"Since the stairway is so old, one can understand that it doesn't look quite the same now as when it was new. I don't know how much they troubled themselves about such matters at that time; but big as it was, no broom could have kept it clean. After a couple of years, moss and lichen began to grow on it and in the autumn dry leaves and dry grass blew down over it; and in the spring it was littered over with falling stones and gravel. And since all these things were left there to mould, they finally gathered so much soil on the steps that not only herbs and grass, but even bushes and trees could take root there.

"But, meantime, a great disparity has arisen between the three steps. The topmost step, which lies nearest Småland, is mostly covered with poor soil and small stones, and no trees except birches and bird-cherry and spruce — which can stand the cold on the heights, and are satisfied with little — can thrive there. One understands best how poor and dry it is there, when one sees how small the field-plots are, and how tiny the numerous cabins. But on the middle step the soil is better and does not lie bound down under such severe cold. This, one can see at a glance, since the trees here are both higher and of finer quality. Here you'll find maple and oak and linden and weeping-birch and hazel trees growing, but no cone-trees to speak of. And it is still more noticeable because of the amount of cultivated land to be found here; and also because the people have great and beautiful houses. On the middle step there are many churches, with large towns around them; and in every way it makes a better and finer appearance than the top step.

"But the very lowest step is the best of all. It is covered with good rich soil; and, where it lies and bathes in the sea, it hasn't the slightest feeling of the Småland chill. Beeches and chestnut and walnut trees thrive down here; and they grow so big that they tower above the church roofs. Here lie also the largest grainfields; the people have not only timber and farming to live by, but they are also occupied with fishing and trading and seafaring. For this reason you will find the most costly residences and the prettiest churches here; and the parishes have developed into villages and cities.

"But this is not all there is to be said of the three steps. For one must realize that when it rains on the roof of the big Småland house, or when the snow melts up there, the water has to go somewhere; and then, naturally, a lot of it is spilled over the big stairway. In the beginning it probably oozed over the whole stairway, big as it was; then cracks appeared in it, and, gradually, the water accustomed itself to flow alongside of it, in well dug-out grooves. And water is water, whatever one does with it. It never has any rest. In one place it cuts and files away, and in another it adds to. These grooves it has dug into vales, and the walls of the vales it has decked with soil; and bushes and trees and vines have clung to them ever since — so thick, and in such profusion that they almost hide the streams they border. But when the streams come to the landings between the steps, they hurl themselves headlong over them; this is why the water comes with such a seething rush that it gathers strength with which to move millwheels and machinery — these, too, have sprung up by every waterfall.

"But this is not all there is to tell of the land with the three steps. Once upon a time up in the big house in Småland there lived a giant, who had grown very old. And it fatigued him, in his extreme age, to be forced to walk down that long stairway in order to catch salmon from the sea. To him it seemed much more suitable that the salmon should come up to him, where he lived.

"Therefore, he went up on the roof of his great house; and there he stood and threw stones down into the Baltic Sea. He threw them with such force that they flew over the whole of Blekinge and dropped into the sea. And when the stones came down, the salmon got so scared that they came up from the Baltic and fled toward the Blekinge streams; ran through the rapids; flung themselves with high leaps over the waterfalls, and stopped.

"How true this is, one can see by the many islands and points that lie along the coast of Blekinge, and which are nothing in the world but the big stones that the giant threw.

"One can also tell because the salmon always go up in the Blekinge streams and work their way through rapids and still water, all the way to Småland.

"That giant is worthy of great thanks and much honour from the Blekinge people; for salmon in the streams, and stone-cutting on the islands — that means work which gives food to many of them even to this day."

CHAPTER EIGHT

BY RONNEBY RIVER

Friday, April first.

NEITHER the wild geese nor Smirre Fox had thought that they should ever run across each other after leaving Skåne. But as it turned out the wild geese happened to take the route over Blekinge, and thither Smirre Fox had also gone.

So far he had kept himself in the northern parts of the province; and since he had not as yet seen any manor parks, or hunting grounds filled with game and dainty young deer, he was more disgruntled than he could say.

One afternoon, while Smirre tramped around in the desolate forest district of Mellanbygden, not far from Ronneby River, he saw a flock of wild geese fly through the air. Instantly he observed that one of the geese was white and then he knew, of course, with whom he had to deal.

Smirre began immediately to hunt the geese — as much for the pleasure of getting a good square meal, as for the desire to be avenged for all the humiliation they had heaped upon him. He saw that they flew eastward until they came to Ronneby River. Then they changed their course, and followed the river toward the south. He understood that they intended to seek a sleeping-place along the river-bank, and he thought that he should be able to get at a pair of them without much trouble. But when Smirre finally discovered the place where the wild geese had taken refuge, he observed they had chosen such a well-protected spot that he couldn't get near to them.

Ronneby River isn't any big or important body of water; nevertheless, it is just as much talked of, because of its pretty shores. At several points it forces its way forward between steep mountain walls that stand straight out of the water, and are entirely overgrown with honeysuckle and bird-cherry, mountain-ash and osier; and there isn't much that can be more delightful than to row out on the little dark river on a pleasant summer day, and look upward at all the soft green that fastens itself to the rugged mountain sides.

But now, when the wild geese and Smirre came to the river, it was cold and blustery spring-winter; all the trees were nude, and there was probably no one who thought the least little bit about the shore being ugly or pretty. The wild geese thanked their good fortune that they had found a sandstrip wide enough for them to stand upon, on a steep mountain wall. Before them rushed the river, which is strong and turbulent in snow-melting time; behind them they had an impassable mountain-rock wall, and overhanging branches screened them. They couldn't have had it better.

The geese were asleep instantly; but the boy couldn't get a wink of sleep. As soon as the sun had disappeared he was seized with a fear of the darkness, and a wilderness-terror, and he began to long for human beings. Where he lay — tucked in under the goose-wing — he could see nothing, and hear only a little; and he thought if any harm were to come to the goosey-gander, he couldn't save him.

He heard noises and rustlings from all directions, and he grew so uneasy that he had to creep from under the wing and seat himself on the ground, beside the goose.

Long-sighted Smirre stood on the mountain summit and looked down upon the wild geese. "You may as well give this pursuit up first as last," he said to himself. "You can't climb such a steep mountain; you can't swim in such a wild torrent; and there isn't the tiniest strip of land below the mountain which leads to the sleeping-place. Those geese are too wise for you. Don't ever bother yourself again to hunt them!"

But Smirre, like all foxes, found it hard to give up an undertaking already begun, and so he laid down on the extremest point of the mountain edge, and never took his eyes off the wild geese. While he lay and watched them, he thought of all the harm they had done him. Yes, it was their fault that he had been driven from Skåne, and had been obliged to move to poverty-stricken Blekinge. He worked himself up to such a pitch, as he lay there, that he wished the wild geese were dead, even if he himself should not have the satisfaction of eating them.

When Smirre's resentment had reached this height, he heard rasping in a large pine close to him, and saw a squirrel come down from the tree hotly pursued by a marten. Neither of them noticed Smirre; and he sat quietly and watched the chase, which went from tree to tree. He looked at the squirrel, who moved among the branches as lightly as though he'd been able to fly. He looked at the marten, who was not so skilled at climbing as the squirrel, but who still ran up and along the branches just as securely as if they had been even paths in the forest. "If I could only climb half as well as either of them," thought the fox, "those creatures down there wouldn't sleep in peace very long!"

As soon as the squirrel had been captured, and the chase was at an end, Smirre walked over to the marten, but stopped two steps away from him, to signify that he did not wish to cheat him of his prey. He greeted the marten in a very friendly manner, and wished him good luck with his catch. Smirre chose his words well — as foxes always do. The marten, on the contrary, who, with his long and slender body, his fine head, his soft skin, and his light brown neckpiece, looked like a little marvel of beauty, but in reality was nothing but a crude forest dweller — hardly answered him. "It surprises me," said Smirre, "that such a fine hunter as you should be satisfied with chasing squirrels when there is much better game within reach." Here he paused; but when the marten only grinned impudently at him, he continued: "Can it be possible that you haven't seen the wild geese that stand under the mountain wall? or are you not a good enough climber to get down to them?"

This time he didn't have to wait for an answer. The marten rushed up to him with back bent, and every separate hair on end. "Have you seen wild geese?" he hissed. "Where are they? Tell me instantly, or I'll bite your neck off!" "But you must remember that I'm twice your size — so be a little polite. I ask nothing better than to show you the wild geese," returned Smirre.

The next instant the marten was on his way down the steep; and while Smirre sat and watched how he swung his snake-like body from branch to branch, he thought: "That pretty tree-hunter has the wickedest heart in all the forest. I believe that the wild geese will have me to thank for a bloody awakening."

But just as Smirre was waiting to hear the geese's death-rattle, he saw the marten tumble from branch to branch — and plump into the river so the water splashed high. Soon thereafter, wings beat loudly and strongly and all the geese went up in a hasty flight.

Smirre intended to hurry after the geese, but he was so curious to know how they had been saved that he sat there until the marten came clambering up. The poor beast was soaked in mud, and stopped every now and then to rub his head with his fore-paws. "Now wasn't that just what I thought — that you were a booby, and would go and tumble into the river?" said Smirre, contemptuously.

"I'm no booby. You don't have to scold me," said the marten. "I sat — all ready — on one of the lowest branches thinking how I should manage to tear a whole lot of geese to pieces, when a little creature, no bigger than a squirrel, jumped up and threw a stone at my head with such force that I fell into the water; and before I had time to pick myself up ——"

The marten didn't have to say any more. He had no audience. Smirre was already a long way off in pursuit of the wild geese.

In the meantime Akka had flown southward in search of a new sleeping-place. There was still a little daylight; and, besides, the half moon hung high in the heavens, so that she could see a little. Luckily, she was well acquainted in these parts, because it had happened more than once that she had been wind-driven to Blekinge when travelling over the Baltic in the spring.

She followed the river as long as she could see it winding through the moon-lit landscape, like a black, shining snake. In this way she came down to Djupafors — where the river first hides itself in an underground channel and then, clear and transparent, as though it were made of glass, rushes down in a narrow cleft, and breaks into bits against the bottom in glittering drops and flying foam. Below the white falls lay a few stones, between which the water rushed away in a wild torrent cataract. Here Mother Akka alighted. This was another good sleeping-place — especially thus late in the evening, when no human beings moved about. At sunset the geese would hardly have been able to camp there, for Djupafors does not lie in any wilderness. On one side of the falls is a paper factory; on the other, which is steep and tree-grown, is Djupadal Park, where people always stroll about on the steep and slippery paths to enjoy the wild stream's rushing movement down in the ravine.

It was about the same here as at the former place; none of the travellers in the least realized that they had come to a pretty and well-known place. They thought rather that it was ghastly and dangerous to stand and sleep on slippery, wet stones, in the middle of a rumbling waterfall. But they had to be content, if only they were protected from carnivorous animals.

The geese fell asleep instantly, while the boy could find no rest in sleep, but sat beside them that he might watch over the goosey-gander.

After a while, Smirre came running along the river-shore. He spied the geese immediately where they stood out in the foaming whirlpools, and understood that he couldn't get at them here, either. Still he couldn't make up his mind to abandon them, but sat down on the shore and looked at them. He felt very much humbled, and thought that his entire reputation as a hunter was at stake.

All of a sudden, he saw an otter come creeping up from

the falls with a fish in his mouth. Smirre approached him but stopped within two steps of him, to show that he didn't wish to take his game from him.

"You're a remarkable one, who can content yourself with catching a fish while the stones are covered with geese!" said Smirre. He was so eager, that he hadn't taken time to choose his words with his usual care. The otter didn't turn his head once in the direction of the river. He was a vagabond — like all otters — and had fished many times by Vomb Lake, and probably knew Smirre Fox. "I know very well how you act when you want to coax away a salmon trout, Smirre," said he.

"Oh! is it you, Gripe?" said Smirre, and was delighted; for he knew that this particular otter was a quick and accomplished swimmer. "I don't wonder that you do not care to look at the wild geese, since you can't manage to get out to them." But the otter, who had swimming-webs between his toes, and a stiff tail, which was as good as an oar, and a skin that was waterproof, didn't wish to have it said of him that there was a waterfall that he wasn't able to manage. He turned toward the stream; as soon as he caught sight of the wild geese, he threw the fish away, rushed down the steep shore and into the river.

If it had been a little later in the spring, so that the nightingales in Djupafors had been at home, they would have sung for many a day of Gripe's struggle with the rapid. For the otter was thrust back by the waves many times, and carried down river; but he fought his way steadily up again. He swam forward in still water; he crawled over stones, and gradually came nearer the wild geese. It was a perilous trip, which might well have earned the right to be sung by the nightingales.

Smirre followed the otter's course with his eyes as well as he could. Presently he saw that the otter was in the act of climbing up to the wild geese. But just then it shrieked shrill and wild. The otter tumbled backward into the water, and was carried away as if he had been a blind kitten. An instant later, there was a great crackling of geese's wings. They rose and flew away to find another sleeping-place.

The otter soon came ashore. He said nothing, but commenced to lick one of his fore-paws. When Smirre sneered at him because he hadn't succeeded, he burst out: "It was not the fault of my swimming-art, Smirre. I had raced all the way over to the geese and was about to climb up to them when a tiny creature came running, and jabbed me in the foot with something sharp. It hurt so, I lost my footing, and then the current took me."

He didn't have to say any more. Smirre was already far off, on his way to the wild geese.

Once again Akka and her flock had to take a night fly. Fortunately, the moon had not gone down; and with the aid of its light, she succeeded in finding another of those sleeping-places which she knew of in that neighbourhood. Again she followed the shining river toward the south. Over Djapadal's manor, and over Ronneby's dark roofs and white waterfalls she flew forward without alighting. But a little south of the city and not far from the sea, lies Ronneby health-spring, with its bath house and spring house; with its big hotel and summer cottages for the spring's guests. All these stand empty and desolate in winter — which the birds know perfectly well; and many are the bird-companies that seek shelter on the deserted buildings' balustrades and balconies during hard storm-times.

Here the wild geese lit on a balcony, and, as usual, they fell asleep at once. The boy, on the contrary, could not sleep because he hadn't cared to creep in under the gooseygander's wing.

The balcony faced south, so the boy had an outlook over the sea. And since he could not sleep, he sat there and saw how pretty it looked when sea and land meet, here in Blekinge.

It so happens that sea and land can meet in many different ways. In some places the land comes down toward the sea with flat, tufted meadows, and the sea meets the land with flying sand, which it piles up into mounds and drifts. It appears as if both disliked each other so much that they only wished to show the poorest they possess. But it can also happen that when the land comes toward the sea it raises a wall of hills in front of it — as though the sea were something dangerous. When the land acts like that, the sea comes up to it with fiery wrath, and beats and roars and lashes against the rocks, and looks as if it would tear the land-hill to pieces.

But in Blekinge it is altogether different when sea and land meet. There the land breaks itself up into points and islands and islets; and the sea divides itself into fiords and bays and sounds; and it is perhaps this which makes it appear as if they must meet in happiness and harmony.

Think now first and foremost of the sea! Far out it lies desolate and empty and big, and has nothing to do but to roll its gray billows. When it comes toward the land, it happens across the first islet. This it immediately overpowers; tears away everything green, and makes it as gray as itself. Then it meets still another islet; this it treats in the same way. And still another — yes, the same thing happens to this also. It is stripped and plundered, as if it had fallen into robbers' hands. Then the islets come nearer and nearer together, and now the sea must understand that the land sends toward it her littlest children, in order to move it to pity. It also grows more friendly the farther in it comes; rolls its waves less high; moderates its storms; lets the green things stay in cracks and crevices; separates itself into small sounds and inlets, and becomes at last so harmless in the land that little boats dare venture out on it. It hardly knows itself — so mild and friendly has it become.

And then think of the hillside! It lies uniform, and looks the same almost everywhere. It consists of flat grain-fields, with one and another birch-grove between, or of long stretches of forest ranges. It appears as if it had thought of nothing but grain and turnips and potatoes and spruce and pine. Then along comes a fiord that cuts far into it. It doesn't mind that, but borders it with birch and alder, just as if it were an ordinary fresh-water lake. Then still another wave comes driving in. Nor does the hillside bother to cringe to this, but it also gets the same dousing as the first one. Then the fiords begin to broaden and separate; they break up fields and woods and then the hillside cannot help but notice them. "I believe it is the sea itself that is coming," says the Hillside, and then it begins to adorn itself. It wreathes itself with blossoms, travels up and down in hills, and throws islands into the sea. It no longer cares about pines and spruces, but casts them off like old everyday clothes, parading later with big oaks and lindens and chestnuts, and with blossoming leafy bowers, and it becomes as gorgeous as a manor-park. And when it meets the sea, it is so changed that it doesn't know itself. All this cannot be seen very well until summertime; but, at any rate, the boy observed how mild and friendly nature was, and he began to feel calmer than he had felt before that night. Then, suddenly, he heard a sharp and ugly yowl from the bath-house park; and when he stood up he saw, in the pale moonlight, a fox standing on the pavement under the balcony. For Smirre had followed the wild geese once more. But on finding the place where they were quartered, he understood that it was impossible to get at them in any way; therefore he had not been able to keep from yowling with chagrin.

When the fox yowled like that, old Akka, the leader-goose, was awakened. Although she could see nothing, she thought she recognized the voice. "Is it you who are out to-night, Smirre?" said she. "Yes," said Smirre, "it is I; and I want to ask what you geese think of the night I have brought you?"

"Do you mean to say that it is you who have sent the marten and otter against us?" asked Akka. "A good turn shouldn't be denied," retorted Smirre. "You once played the goose-game with me, now I have begun to play the fox-game with you; and I'm not inclined to let up on it so long as a single one of you still lives, even if I have to follow you the world over!"

"You, Smirre, ought at least to think whether it is right for you, who are weaponed with both teeth and claws, to hound us in this way; we, who are defenceless," said Akka.

Smirre thought that Akka sounded scared, and he promptly said: "If you, Akka, will take that Thumbietot, who has so often opposed me, and throw him down to me, I'll promise to make my peace with you. Then I'll never more pursue you or any of yours." "I'm not going to give you Thumbietot," said Akka. "From the youngest of us to the oldest, we would willingly give our lives for his sake!" "Since you're so fond of him," said Smirre, "I promise you that he shall be the first among you that I will wreak vengeance upon."

Akka said no more, and after Smirre had sent up a few more yowls, all was still. The boy lay all the while awake. Now it was Akka's words to the fox that prevented his sleeping. Never had he dreamed that he should hear anything so great as that some one was willing to risk life for his sake. From that moment, it could no longer be said of Nils Holgersson that he cared for no one.

CHAPTER NINE

KARLSKRONA

Saturday, April third.

IT WAS a moonlight evening in Karlskrona — calm and beautiful. But earlier in the day there had been rain and wind; and the people must have thought that the bad weather still continued, for hardly a soul had ventured out into the streets.

While the city lay there so desolate, Akka, the wild goose, and her flock, came flying toward it over Vemmön and Pantarholmen. They were out in the late evening to seek a sleeping-place on the islands. They couldn't remain inland because they were disturbed by Smirre Fox wherever they lighted.

As the boy rode along, high up in the air, and looked at the sea and the islands which spread before him, he thought that everything appeared so strange and spooky. The heavens were no longer blue, but encased him like a globe of green glass. The sea was milk-white, and as far as he could see rolled small white waves tipped with silver ripples. In among all this white lay numerous little islets, coal black. Whether they were big or little, whether they were even as meadows, or full of cliffs, they looked just as black. Even dwelling-houses and churches and windmills, which at other times are white or red, were now outlined in black against the green sky. The boy thought it was as if the earth had been transformed, and he was come to another world.

He felt that just for this one night he wanted to be brave, and not afraid — when he saw something that really frightened him. It was a high cliff island, covered with big, angular blocks; and between the dark blocks glittered specks of bright, shining gold. He couldn't keep from thinking of Maglestone, by Trolle-Ljungby, which the trolls sometimes raised upon high golden pillars; and he wondered if this wasn't something of the same sort.

It would have been well enough with the stones and the gold if there hadn't been so many fiendish things all around the island. They looked like whales and sharks and other big sea-monsters. But the boy understood that these were sea-trolls, who had gathered around the island and intended to crawl up on it, to fight with the land-trolls who lived there. And those on the land were probably afraid, for he saw how a big giant stood on the highest point of the island and raised his arms, as if in despair over all the misfortune that was to come to him and to his island.

The boy was not a little terrified when he noticed that Akka began to descend right over that particular island! "No, for pity's sake! We must not light there," gasped he.

But the geese continued the descent and soon the boy was astonished that he could have seen things so awry. In the first place, the big stone blocks were nothing but houses. The whole island was a city; and the shining gold specks were street lamps and lighted window-panes. The giant standing on the topmost point of the island with his arms raised was a church with two cross-towers; all the sea-trolls and monsters, which he thought he had seen, were boats and ships of every description, lying at anchor all around the island. On the land side they were mostly row-boats and sail-boats and small coast steamers; but on the side that faced the sea lay armour-clad battleships; some were broad, with thick, slanting smoke-stacks; others were long and narrow and so constructed that they could glide through the water like fishes.

Now what city might this be? That, the boy could guess because he saw all the battleships. All his life he had loved ships, although he had had nothing to do with any, except the galleys which he had sailed in the road ditches. He knew well that this city, where so many battleships lay, could only be Karlskrona.

The boy's grandfather had been an old marine; and all his life, he had talked of Karlskrona — of the great warship dock, and of all the other things to be seen in that city. The boy felt perfectly at home, and was glad that he was going to see all of which he had heard so much.

But he had only had a glimpse of the towers and fortifications which barred the entrance to the harbour, and the many buildings, and the shipyard, when Akka sank down to one of the flat church-towers.

This was a pretty safe place for those who wanted to get away from a fox, and the boy began to wonder if he couldn't venture to crawl in under the goosey-gander's wing for this one night. Yes, that he might safely do. It would do him good to get a little sleep. He would try to see more of the dock and the ships at daybreak.

It seemed strange to the boy that he could keep still and wait until morning to see the ships. He certainly had not slept five minutes before he slipped out from under the wing and slid down the lightning-rod and the water-spout all the way to the ground.

Presently he stood on a big square in front of the church. It was paved with round stones, and for him it was just as hard to walk there as it is for big people to walk on a tufted meadow. Those who are accustomed to live in the open, or far out in the country, always feel uneasy when they come into a city, where the houses stand straight and forbidding, and the streets are open, so that every one can see who goes there. And it happened in the same way with the boy. When he stood on the big Karlskrona square, and looked at the German church, the town hall, and the cathedral from which he had just descended, he wished himself back on the tower with the geese.

It was a lucky thing that the square was entirely deserted. There wasn't a human being about — unless a statue on its high pedestal could be counted in. The boy stared long at the statue, which represented a big, brawny man in a three-cornered hat, long waistcoat, knee-breeches, and coarse shoes — and wondered who he was. The man held a long stick in his hand, and he looked as if he would know how to make use of it, too — for he had an awfully severe countenance, with a big, hooked nose and an ugly mouth.

"What is that long-lipped thing doing here?" the boy cried at last. Never had he felt so small and insignificant as he did that night. He tried to jolly himself up a bit by saying something audacious. Then he thought no more about the statue, but betook himself to a wide street which led down to the sea.

The boy hadn't gone far when he heard some one following him. Somebody was walking behind him, who stamped on the stone pavement with heavy footsteps and pounded on the ground with a hard stick. It sounded as if the big bronze man up in the square had started on a tramp.

The boy listened for the steps as he ran down the street, and he became more and more convinced that it was the bronze man. The ground trembled, and the houses shook. It couldn't be any one but he who walked so heavily. The boy became panic-stricken as he thought of what he had just said to him. He did not dare turn his head to find out if it really was he.

"Perhaps he is only out for a walk," thought the boy. "Surely he can't be angry at me for the words I spoke. They were not at all badly meant."

Instead of going straight on, and trying to get down to the dock, the boy turned into a side street leading east. First and last he wanted to get away from the one who tramped after him.

But the next instant the bronze man turned down the same street; and then the boy was so scared that he didn't know what to do with himself. And how hard it was to find any hiding-places in a city where all the gates were closed! Then to the right, a short distance from the street, he saw an old frame church, in the centre of a large grove. Not an instant did he pause to consider, but hurried on toward the church. "If I can only get there, then I'll surely be shielded from all harm," thought he.

As he ran on he suddenly caught sight of a man standing on a gravel path beckoning to him. "*There* is certainly some one who will help me!" thought the boy. Oh, how relieved he felt! And he hurried off in the man's direction. He was actually so frightened that the heart of him fairly thumped in his breast.

But when he got up to the man, who stood at the edge of the gravel path, upon a low pedestal, he was absolutely thunderstruck. "Surely, it can't be that one who beckoned to me!" he thought; for he saw that the entire man was made of wood.

The boy stood there and stared at him. He was a thickset man on short legs, with a broad, ruddy countenance, shiny, black hair and full black beard. On his head he wore a wooden hat; on his body, a brown wooden coat; around his waist, a black wooden belt; on his legs he had wide wooden knee-breeches and wooden stockings; and on his feet black wooden shoes. He was newly painted and newly varnished, so that he glistened and shone in the moonlight. He looked so good-natured that the boy at once placed confidence in him.

In his left hand he held a wooden slate, and there the boy read:

>Most humbly I beg you,
> Though voice I may lack.
>Come drop a penny, do;
> But lift my hat!

Oho! so the man was only a poor-box. The boy felt that he had been fooled. He had expected this to be something really remarkable. And now he remembered that grandpa had also spoken of the wooden man, and had said that all the children in Karlskrona were very fond of him. And that must have been true, for he, too, found it hard to part with the wooden man. He had something so old-timey about him, that one could well take him to be many hundred years old; and at the same time, he looked so strong and bold, and spirited — just as one might imagine that folks looked in olden times.

The boy had so much fun gazing at the wooden man, that he entirely forgot the one from whom he was fleeing. But now he heard him turning from the street into the churchyard. So he had followed him here, too! Where could the boy go?

Just then he saw the wooden man bend down to him and stretch forth his big, brown hand. It was impossible to think anything but good of him; and with one jump, the boy stood in his hand. The wooden man lifted him to his hat — and stuck him under it.

The boy was just hidden, and the wooden man had just got his arm back to its right place again, when the bronze man stopped in front of him and banged the stick on the ground so that the wooden man shook on his pedestal. Thereupon the bronze man said in a strong and resonant voice: "Who might you be?"

The wooden man's arm went up, so that it creaked in the old woodwork, and he touched his hat-brim as he replied: "Rosenbom, by Your Majesty's leave. Once upon a time boatswain on the man-of-war, *Audacity;* after completed service, sexton at the Admiral's Church — and, lately, carved in wood and exhibited in the churchyard as a poor-box."

The boy gave a start when he heard the wooden man say "Your Majesty." For now, as he thought about it, he knew that the statue on the square represented the one who founded the city. It was probably no one less than Charles the Eleventh himself that he had encountered.

"You give a good account of yourself," said the bronze man. "Can you also tell me if you have seen a little brat who runs around in the city to-night? He's an impudent rascal, and if I get hold of him, I'll teach him manners!" With that, he again pounded on the ground with his stick, and looked fearfully angry.

"By Your Majesty's leave, I have seen him," said the wooden man; and the boy was so scared that he commenced to shake where he sat under the hat and looked at the bronze man through a crack in the wood. But he calmed down when the wooden man continued: "Your Majesty is on the wrong track. That youngster certainly intended to run into the shipyard, to hide there."

"You don't tell me, Rosenbom? Well then, don't stand on the pedestal any longer but come with me and help me find him. Four eyes are better than two, Rosenbom."

But the wooden man answered in a doleful voice: "I would most humbly beg to be permitted to stay where I am. I look well and sleek because of the paint, but I'm old and mouldy, and cannot stand moving about."

The bronze man was not one who liked to be contradicted. "What sort of notions are these? Come along, Rosenbom!" Then he raised his stick and gave him a resounding whack on his wooden shoulder. "Does Rosenbom not see that he holds together?"

With that the two set out together — big and mighty — on the streets of Karlskrona — till they came to a high gate, which led to the shipyard. Just outside and on guard walked one of the navy's jacktars, but the bronze man strutted past him and kicked the gate open without the jacktar's pretending to notice it.

As soon as they got into the shipyard, they saw before them a wide, expansive harbour separated by pile-bridges. In the different harbour basins lay the warships, which looked bigger, and more awe-inspiring than when the boy had seen them from above. "Then it wasn't so crazy after all to imagine that they were sea-trolls," thought he.

"Where does Rosenbom think it most advisable for us to begin the search?" said the bronze man.

"One like him could very easily conceal himself in the hall of models," replied the wooden man.

Ancient structures lay all along the harbour on a narrow strip of land which stretched to the right from the gate.

The bronze man walked over to a building with low walls, small windows, and a conspicuous roof. He pounded on the door with his stick until it burst open; then tramped up a pair of worn-out steps. Soon they came into a large hall which was filled with tackled and full-rigged little ships. The boy understood without being told that they were models for the ships which had been built for the Swedish navy. There were many different varieties. Some were old men-of-war, whose sides bristled with cannon, and had high structures fore and aft — their masts weighed down with a network of sails and ropes. There were small island-boats with rowing-benches along the sides; there were undecked cannon sloops and richly gilded frigates, which were models of the ones the kings had used on their travels. Finally, there were also the heavy, broad armour-plated ships with towers and cannon on deck — such as are in use nowadays; and narrow, shining torpedo boats which resembled long, slender fishes.

While the boy was being carried around among all this, he was awed. "Fancy that such big, splendid ships have been built here in Sweden!" he thought to himself.

He had plenty of time to see all that was to be seen. For when the bronze man saw the models, he forgot everything else, and examined them from the first to the last, and asked about them. Rosenbom, the boatswain on the *Audacity*, told as much as he knew of the ships' builders, and of those who had manned them; and of the fates they had met. He told of Chapman and Puke and Trolle; of Hoagland

and Svensksund — all the way along until 1809 — after that he had not been there.

Both he and the bronze man had the most to say about the fine old wooden ships. The new battleships they didn't exactly appear to understand.

"I can see that Rosenbom doesn't know anything about these new-fangled things," said the bronze man. "Therefore, let us go and look at something else; for this amuses me, Rosenbom."

By this time he had entirely given up his search for the boy, who felt calm and secure where he sat in the wooden hat.

Thereupon both men wandered through the big establishment: sail-making shops, anchor smithy, machine and carpenter shops. They saw the mast sheers and the docks; the large magazines, the arsenal, the rope-bridge and the big discarded dock, which had been blasted in the bed-rock. They went out upon the pile-bridges, where the naval vessels lay moored, stepped on board and examined them like two old sea-dogs; wondered; disapproved; approved; and became indignant.

The boy sat in safety under the wooden hat, and heard all about how they had laboured and struggled in this place to equip the navies which had gone out from here. He heard how life and blood had been risked; how the last penny had been sacrificed to build the warships; how men of genius had strained all their powers, in order to perfect these ships which had been their Fatherland's safeguard. A couple of times the tears came to the boy's eyes, as he heard all this.

And last, they went into an open court where the galley models of old men-of-war were grouped; and a more curious sight the boy had never beheld; for these models had inconceivably powerful and terror-striking faces. They were big, fearless and savage: filled with the same proud spirit that had fitted out the great ships. They were from another time than his. He fancied that he shrivelled up before them.

But when they came in here, the bronze man said to the wooden man: "Take off thy hat, Rosenbom, for those that stand here! They have all fought for the Fatherland."

And Rosenbom, like the bronze man, had forgotten why they had begun this tramp. Without thinking, he lifted the wooden hat from his head and shouted:

"I take off my hat to the one who chose the harbour and founded the shipyard and recreated the navy; to the monarch who has awakened all this into life!"

"Thanks, Rosenbom! That was well spoken. Rosenbom is a fine man. But what is this, Rosenbom?"

For there stood Nils Holgersson, right on the top of Rosenbom's bald pate. He was no longer afraid but doffed his white toboggan hood, and shouted: "Hurrah for you, Longlip!"

The bronze man struck the ground hard with his stick; but the boy never learned what he had intended to do to him, for now the sun ran up, and straightway both the bronze man and the wooden man vanished — as if they had been made of mists. While he still stood staring after them, the wild geese flew from the church tower, and circled back and forth over the city. Presently they caught sight of Nils; and then the big white one darted down from the sky and fetched him.

CHAPTER TEN

THE TRIP TO ÖLAND

Sunday, April third.

THE wild geese went out on a wooded island to feed. There they happened to run across a few gray geese who were surprised to see them — since they knew very well that their kinsmen, the wild geese, usually travel over the interior of the country.

They were curious and inquisitive, and wouldn't be satisfied with less than the wild geese telling them all about the hounding which they had to take from Smirre Fox. When they had finished, a gray goose, who appeared to be as old and as wise as Akka herself, said: "It was a great misfortune for you that Smirre Fox was declared an outlaw in his own land. He'll be sure to keep his word, and follow you all the way up to Lapland. If I were in your place, I shouldn't travel north over Småland. I should take the outside route over Öland instead, to throw him off the track entirely. To really mislead him, you must remain for a couple of days on Öland's southern point. There you'll find lots of food and lots of company. I don't think you'll regret it, if you go over there."

This was certainly sensible advice, and the wild geese concluded to take it. As soon as they had eaten all they could hold, they started on the journey to Oland. None of them had ever been there before, but the gray goose had given them careful directions. They only had to travel straight south until they came to a large bird-track, which extended all along the Blekinge Coast. All the birds who had winter homes by the West Coast and were now on their way to Finland and Russia flew forward there — and, in passing, they were always in the habit of stopping at Oland to rest. The wild geese would have no trouble in finding guides.

That day it was perfectly still and warm, like a summer's day — the best weather in the world for a sea trip. The only drawback was that it was not quite clear, for the skies were gray and veiled. Here and there were enormous clouds which hung far down to the sea's outer edge, obstructing the view.

When the travellers had passed beyond the rock-islands, the sea spread out so smooth and mirror-like that, as the boy looked down, he thought the water had disappeared. There was no longer any earth under him. He had only mist and sky around him. He grew very dizzy, and held himself tight on the goose-back — more frightened than when he sat there for the first time. It seemed as if he couldn't possibly hold on, but must fall in some direction.

It was even worse when they reached the big bird-track, of which the gray goose had spoken. Flock after flock came flying in exactly the same direction. They seemed to follow a fixed route. There were ducks and gray geese, surf-scoters and guillemots, loons and pin-tail ducks and mergansers and grebes and oyster-catchers and sea-grouse. But now, when the boy leaned forward and looked in the direction where the sea ought to lie, he saw the entire bird procession reflected in the water. But he was so dizzy that he didn't understand how this had come about: he thought that all the birds flew with their bellies upside down. Still he didn't wonder so much at this, for he did not himself know which was up and which was down.

The birds were tired out and impatient to get on. Not one of them shrieked or said a funny thing, and this made everything seem peculiarly unreal.

"Think, if we have travelled away from the earth!" he said to himself. "Think, if we are on our way up to heaven!"

He saw nothing but mists and birds around him, and began to look upon it as reasonable that they were travelling heavenward. He was glad, and wondered what he should see up there. The dizziness passed all at once. He was so exceedingly happy in the thought that he was on his way to heaven and was leaving this earth.

Just about then he heard a couple of loud shots, and saw two white smoke-columns rise.

There was a sudden awakening and an unrest among the birds. "Hunters! Hunters!" they cried. "Fly high! Fly away!"

Then the boy finally saw that they were travelling all the while over the seacoast and that they were certainly not in heaven. In a long row lay small boats filled with hunters, who fired shot upon shot. The nearest bird-flocks hadn't noticed them in time. They had flown too low. Several dark bodies sank down toward the sea; and for every one that fell there arose cries of anguish from the living.

It was strange for one who had but lately believed himself in heaven to wake up suddenly to such fear and lamentation. Akka shot toward the heights and the flock followed with the greatest possible speed. The wild geese got safely out of the way, but the boy couldn't get over his amazement. "To think that any one could wish to shoot at such as Akka and Yksi and Kaksi and the goosey-gander and the others! Human beings had no conception of what they did."

So it bore on again, in the still air, and all was as quiet as before, but for some of the tired birds calling out every now and then: "Are we not there soon? Are you sure we're on the right track?" Whereupon, the leaders answered: "We are travelling straight to Öland; straight to Oland."

The gray geese were tired out, and the loons circled around them. "Don't be in such a rush!" cried the ducks. "You'll eat up all the food before we get there." "Oh! there'll be enough for all of us," answered the loons.

Before they had gone far enough to sight Oland, a light wind blew against them. It brought with it something that looked like immense clouds of white smoke — as if there was a big fire somewhere.

When the birds saw the first white spiral haze, they became uneasy and increased their speed. But that which resembled smoke blew thicker and thicker, and at last it enveloped them altogether. There was no odour of smoke; and this smoke was not dark and dry, but white and damp. Suddenly the boy realized that it was only a mist.

When the mist became so thick that they couldn't see a goose-length ahead, the birds began to carry on like real lunatics. All who before had travelled forward in such perfect order now began to play in the mist. They flew hither and thither to entice one another astray. "Be careful!" they cried. "You're only travelling round and round. Turn back, for pity's sake! You'll never get to Öland that way."

They all knew perfectly well where the island was, but they tried their best to lead each other astray. "Look at those wagtails!" rang out in the mist. "They are going back toward the North Sea!" "Have a care, wild geese!" shrieked some one from another direction. "If you continue like this, you'll get clear up to Rügen."

There was of course no danger that the birds who were accustomed to travel here would permit themselves to be lured in a wrong direction. But the ones who had a hard time of it were the wild geese! The jesters observed that they were uncertain as to the way, and did all they could to confuse them.

"Where are you bound for, good people?" called a swan. He came right up to Akka, looking sympathetic and serious.

"We are travelling to Öland; we have never been there before," said Akka. She thought that here was a bird to be trusted.

"It's too bad," said the swan, "they have lured you in the wrong direction. You're on the road to Blekinge. Now come with me, and I'll put you right!"

So he flew off with them, and when he had taken them so far away from the track that they could hear no calls, he disappeared in the mist.

They flew around a while at random. They had barely succeeded in tracking the birds when a duck approached them. "You'd better lie down on the water until the mist clears," said the duck. "It is evident that you are not accustomed to looking out for yourself on journeys."

Those rogues succeeded in making Akka's head swim. As near as the boy could make out, the wild geese circled round and round for a long time.

"Be careful! Can't you see that you are flying up and down?" shouted a loon as he rushed by.

The boy positively clutched the goosey-gander around

the neck. This was something which he had feared for a long time.

If they had not heard a rolling and muffled sound in the distance, no one could have told when they would have arrived.

Then Akka craned her neck, snapped hard with her wings, and rushed on at full speed. Now she had something to go by. The gray goose had told her not to light on Öland's southern point, because there was a cannon there, which the people used to shoot at the mist. Now she knew the way, and now no one in the world could lead her astray.

Chapter Eleven

OLAND'S SOUTHERN POINT

April, third to sixth.

ON THE most southerly part of Oland lies a royal demesne, called Ottenby. It is a rather large estate which extends from shore to shore, straight across the island; and it is remarkable in that it has always been a haunt for large bird-companies.

In the Seventeenth Century, when the kings used to go over to Oland to hunt, the entire estate was simply a deer park. In the Eighteenth Century there was a stud there, where blooded race-horses were bred; and a sheep farm, where hundreds of sheep were maintained. In our day you'll find neither blooded horses nor sheep at Ottenby, but great herds of young horses, which are to be used by the cavalry. And in all the land there could be no better abode for animals.

Along the extreme eastern shore lies the old sheep meadow which is a mile and a half long, and the largest meadow in all Oland. There animals can graze and play and run about as free as if they were in a wilderness. And there you will find the celebrated Ottenby Grove with the hundred-year-old oaks, which give shade from the sun, and shelter from the severe Oland winds. And we must not forget the long Ottenby wall, which stretches from shore to shore and separates Ottenby from the rest of the island, so that the animals may know how far the old royal demesne extends and be careful about getting in on other ground, where they are not so well protected.

You'll find plenty of tame animals at Ottenby, but that isn't all. One could almost believe that the wild ones also felt that on an old crown property both wild and tame creatures can count upon shelter and protection — since they venture there in such great numbers.

Besides, there are still a few stags of the old stock left; and burrow-ducks, and partridges love to live there, and it offers a resting place in spring and late summer for thousands of migratory birds. Above all, it is on the swampy eastern shore below the sheep meadow where the migratory birds alight to rest and feed.

When the wild geese and Nils had finally found their way to Öland, they came down, like all the rest, on the shore near the sheep meadow. The mist lay thick over the island, as well as over the sea. But still the boy was amazed at all the birds which he discovered only on the little narrow stretch of shore which he could see.

It was a low sand-shore with stones and pools, and heaps of cast-up seaweed. If the boy had been allowed to choose, it isn't likely that he would have thought of alighting there; but the birds probably looked upon this as a veritable paradise. Ducks and geese walked about and fed on the meadow; nearer to the water ran snipe, and other coast-birds. The loons lay in the sea and fished, but the greatest life and movement was upon the seaweed banks along the coast. There the birds stood side by side close together and gobbled grub-worms which must have been found there in limitless numbers, for it was very evident that there was never any complaint over a lack of food.

The great majority were going to travel farther, and had

only alighted to take a short rest; and as soon as the leader of a flock thought his comrades sufficiently refreshed he said: "If you are ready now, we may as well move on."

"No, wait, wait! We haven't had anything like enough," cried the company.

"You surely don't believe that I intend to let you eat so much that you will not be able to move?" said the leader, flapping his wings and starting off. Along the outermost seaweed banks lay a flock of swans. They didn't bother to go on land, but rested themselves by lying and rocking on the water. Now and then they would thrust their necks under the water and bring up food from the sea-bottom. When they got hold of anything very good, they indulged in loud shouts that sounded like trumpet calls.

When the boy heard that there were swans on the shoals, he hurried out to the seaweed banks. He had never before seen wild swans at close range. He had the good luck to get quite close to them.

The boy was not the only one who had heard the swans. Wild geese, gray geese and loons swam out between the banks, formed a ring around the swans and stared at them. The swans ruffled their feathers, raised their wings like sails, and stretched their necks high in the air. Occasionally one and another of them swam up to a goose, or a great loon, or a diving-duck, and said a few words. And then it appeared as though the one addressed hardly dared raise his bill to reply.

But there was a little loon — a tiny mischievous baggage — that couldn't stand all this ceremony. He made a quick dive, and disappeared. Soon after that, one of the swans let out a scream, and swam off so quickly that the water foamed. Then he stopped and began to look majestic once more. Presently another one shrieked in the same way as the first one, and then a third.

The little loon wasn't able to stay under water any longer, but bobbed up to the water's edge, little and black and venomous. The swans rushed toward him; but when they saw what a poor little wretch it was, they turned abruptly — as if they considered themselves too good to quarrel with him. Then the little loon dived again, and pinched their feet. It certainly must have hurt; but the worst was that they could not maintain their dignity. At once they took a decided stand. They began to beat the air with their wings so that it thundered, came forward a bit — as if running on the water — finally they got wind under their wings, and rose.

When the swans were gone they were greatly missed; and those who had but lately been amused by the little loon's antics scolded him for his thoughtlessness.

The boy walked back toward firm land again, where he stationed himself to watch the pool-snipe play. They resembled small storks, and like these, had small bodies, tall legs, long necks, and light, swaying movements; only they were not gray, but brown. They stood in a long row on the shore where it was washed by waves. As soon as a wave rolled in, the whole row ran backward; as soon as it receded, they followed it. And they kept this up for hours.

The showiest of all the birds were the burrow-ducks. They were undoubtedly related to the ordinary ducks; for, like these, they too had a thick-set body, a broad bill, and webbed feet; but they were much more elaborately gotten up. The feather dress itself was white; around the neck they wore a broad gold band; the wing-mirror shimmered in green, red, and black; the wing-tips were black, the head was a dark green and shone like satin.

As soon as any of these appeared on the shore, the others would say: "Now just look at those freaks! They know how to tog themselves out." "If they were not so conspicuous, they wouldn't have to dig their nests in the earth, but could lie above ground, like any one else," said a brown mallard-duck. "They may try as much as they please, but they'll never get anywhere with such noses," remarked a gray goose. And this was actually true. The burrow-ducks have a big knob at the base of the bill, which spoils their appearance.

Close to the shore, sea-gulls and sea-swallows moved forward in the water, and fished. "What kind of fish are you catching?" asked a wild goose. "Stickleback! — Öland stickleback. It's the best stickleback in the world," said a gull. "Won't you taste of it?" And he flew up to the goose with his mouth full of the little fishes, and wanted to give her some. "Ugh! Do you think that I eat such filth?" said the wild goose in disgust.

The next morning it was just as cloudy. The wild geese walked about on the meadow and fed; but the boy had gone to the seashore to gather mussels. There were plenty of them; and when he thought that the next day, perhaps, they would be in some place where they couldn't get any food at all, he determined that he would try to make himself a little bag, which he could fill with mussels. He found an old sedge on the meadow which was strong and tough; and out of this he began to braid a knapsack. He worked at it for several hours, but when finished he was well satisfied with it.

At dinner time all the wild geese came running and asked him if he had seen anything of the white goosey-gander. "No, he has not been with me," said the boy. "We had him with us all along until just lately," said Akka, "but now we no longer know where he's to be found."

The boy jumped up, and was terribly frightened. He asked if any fox or eagle had put in an appearance, or if any human being had been seen in the neighbourhood. But no one had noticed anything dangerous. The goosey-gander had probably lost his way in the mist.

But to the boy the misfortune was just as great no matter how the white one had been lost, and he started off immediately to hunt for him. The mist shielded him, so that he could run wherever he wished without being seen, but it also prevented him from seeing. He ran southward along the shore — all the way down to the lighthouse and the mist cannon on the island's extreme point. There was the same bird confusion everywhere, but no goosey-gander. He ventured over to Ottenby estate, and he searched every one of the old, hollow oaks in Ottenby grove, but he found no trace of the goosey-gander.

He searched until it began to grow dark. Then he had to turn back to the eastern shore. He walked with heavy steps and was fearfully blue. He didn't know what would become of him if he couldn't find the goosey-gander. There was no one whom he could spare less.

But what was that big, white object coming toward him in the mist if it wasn't the goosey-gander? He was all right, and very glad that at last he had been able to find his way back to the others. The mist had made him so dizzy, he said, that he had wandered around on the big meadow all day long. The boy threw his arms around his neck, for very joy, and begged him to take care of himself and not to wander away from the others. And he promised, positively, that he never would do so again. No, never again.

But next morning, when the boy was walking along the beach looking for mussels, the geese came running and asked if he had seen the goosey-gander. No, of course he hadn't. "Well, then, the goosey-gander was lost again. He had gone astray in the mist, just as on the day before."

The boy ran off in great alarm and began to search. He found one place where the Ottenby wall was so tumbledown that he could climb over it. Later he went about on the shore — which gradually widened and became so large that there was room for fields and meadows and farms — then up on the flat highland, which lay in the middle of the island, where there were no buildings except windmills, and where the turf was so thin that the white cement shone through it.

Meanwhile, he could not find the goosey-gander; and as it was drawing on toward evening and the boy must return to the beach, he couldn't believe anything but that his travelling companion was lost. He was so depressed, he did not know what to do with himself.

He had already clambered over the wall again, when he heard a crash close beside him. As he turned to see what it was that had fallen, he distinguished something that moved on a stone-heap close to the wall. He stole nearer, and saw the goosey-gander come trudging wearily over the stone-heap, with several long fibres in his mouth. The goosey-gander did not see the boy, and the boy did not call to him, but thought it advisable to find out first why the goosey-gander time and again disappeared in this manner.

And he soon learned the cause of it. Up in the stone-heap

lay a young gray goose, who cried with joy when the goosey-gander came. The boy crept near to them, so that he heard what they said. Then he found out that the gray goose was wounded in one wing, so that she could not fly, and that her flock had flown away and had left her all alone. She was near death's door with hunger, when the white goosey-gander heard her call, the other day, and sought her out. Ever since, he had been carrying food to her. Both of them hoped that she would be well before his flock left the island, but, as yet, she could neither fly nor walk. She was very much worried over this, but he comforted her with the thought that he shouldn't travel for a long time. At last he bade her good-night, and promised to come the next day.

The boy let the goosey-gander go; and as soon as he was gone, he, in turn, stole up to the stone-heap. He was angry because he had been deceived, and now he wanted to say to that gray goose that the goosey-gander was his property. He was going to take the boy up to Lapland, and there would be no talk of his staying here on her account. But now, when he saw the young gray goose close to, he understood not only why the goosey-gander had gone and carried food to her for two days, but also why he had not wished to mention the fact that he had helped her. She had the prettiest little head; her feather-dress was like soft satin, and her eyes were mild and pleading.

When she saw the boy, she wanted to run away; but the left wing was out of joint and dragged on the ground, so that it interfered with her movements.

"You mustn't be afraid of me," said the boy, and didn't look nearly so angry as he had intended to appear. "I'm Thumbietot, Morten Goosey-gander's comrade," he announced. Then he stood there, and didn't know what he wanted to say.

Occasionally one finds something among animals which makes one wonder what sort of creatures they really are. One is almost afraid that they may be transformed human beings. It was something like this with the gray goose. As soon as Thumbietot said who he was, she lowered her neck and head very charmingly before him, and said in a voice so sweet that he couldn't believe it was a goose that spoke: "I am very glad that you have come here to help me. The white goosey-gander has told me that no one is so wise and so good as you."

She said this with such dignity that the boy grew really embarrassed. "This surely can't be any bird," thought he. "It is certainly some bewitched princess."

He was filled with a desire to help her, and ran his hand under the feathers, and felt along the wing-bone. The bone was not broken, but there was something wrong with the joint. He put his finger down into the empty socket. "Be careful, now!" he said, as he got a firm grip on the bone-pipe and fitted it into the place where it ought to be. He did it rather quickly and well, considering it was the first time that he had attempted anything of the sort. But it must have hurt very much, for the poor young goose uttered a shrill cry, then sank down among the stones without showing a sign of life.

The boy was terribly frightened. He had only wished to help her, and now she was dead. He made a big jump from the stone-heap, and ran away. He thought it was as though he had murdered a human being.

The next morning the air was clear and free from mist, and Akka said that now they should continue their journey.

All the others were willing to go, but the white goosey-gander made excuses. The boy understood well enough that he didn't care to leave the gray goose. Akka did not listen to him, but started off.

The boy jumped upon the goosey-gander's back, and the white one followed the flock — albeit slowly and unwillingly. The boy was mighty glad that they could fly away from the island. He was conscience-stricken on account of the gray goose, and didn't want to tell the goosey-gander what had happened when he had tried to cure her. It would probably be best if Morten Goosey-gander never found out about this, he thought, though he wondered, at the same time, how the white one had the heart to leave the gray goose.

But suddenly the goosey-gander turned. The thought of the young gray goose had overpowered him. It could go as it would with the Lapland trip: he couldn't go with the others when he knew that she was alone and ill, and would starve to death. A few wing-strokes and he was over by the stone-heap, but now there lay no young gray goose between the stones. "Dunfin! Dunfin! Where art thou?" called the goosey-gander.

"The fox has probably been here and taken her," thought the boy. But at that moment he heard a sweet voice answer the goosey-gander. "Here am I, goosey-gander; here am I! I have only been taking a morning bath." And up from the water came the little gray goose — fresh and in good trim — and told how Thumbietot had pulled her wing into place, and how she was entirely well, and ready to go with them on the journey.

The drops of water lay like pearl-dew on her shimmery satin-like feathers, and again Thumbietot thought that she was a real little princess.

Chapter Twelve

THE BIG BUTTERFLY

Wednesday, April sixth.

THE geese flew ahead over the long island which lay distinctly visible under them. The boy felt happy and light of heart during the trip. He was just as pleased and contented now as he had been glum and depressed the day before, when he roamed around on the island hunting for the goosey-gander.

He saw now that the interior of the island consisted of a barren high plain, with a wreath of fertile land along the coast; and he began to comprehend the meaning of something which he had heard the other evening.

He had just seated himself by one of the many windmills on the highland to rest a bit, when a couple of shepherds came along with their dogs beside them, and a large flock of sheep in their train. The boy was not afraid since he was well hidden under the windmill steps. But it so happened that the shepherds came and seated themselves on the same steps, and then there was nothing for him to do but keep perfectly still.

One of the shepherds was young, and looked about as folks do mostly; the other was an old queer one. His body was large and knotty, but the head was small, and the face had sensitive and delicate features It appeared as though the body and head didn't belong together.

He sat silent a while, gazing into the mist with an unutterably weary expression. Then he began to talk to his companion. Presently the other took from his knapsack some bread and cheese, to eat his evening meal. He answered almost nothing, but listened very patiently, as if he were thinking: "I may as well give you the pleasure of chattering a while."

"Now I shall tell you something, Eric," said the old shepherd. "I have figured out that in former days, when both human beings and animals were much larger than now, that the butterflies, too, must have been uncommonly large. And there was once a butterfly that was many miles long, and had wings as wide as seas. Those wings were blue, and shone like silver, and so gorgeous that, when the butterfly was out flying, all the other animals stood still and stared at it. It had this drawback, however, that it was too large. The wings had hard work to carry it. But probably all would have gone very well if the butterfly had been wise enough to remain on the hillside. But it wasn't; it ventured out over the Baltic Sea. And it hadn't got very far before the storm came along and began to tear at its wings. Well, it's easy to understand, Eric, how things would go when the Baltic Sea storm began to wrestle with frail butterfly-wings. It wasn't long before they were torn away and scattered; and then, of course, the poor butterfly fell into the sea. At first it was tossed back and forth on the billows, and then stranded upon a few cliff-foundations just beyond Småland. And there it lay — large and long as it was.

"Now I think, Eric, that if the butterfly had dropped on land, it would soon have rotted and fallen apart. But since it fell into the sea, it was soaked through and through with lime, and became as hard as a stone. You know, of course, that we have found stones on the shore which are nothing but petrified worms. Now I believe that it went the same way with the big butterfly-body. I believe that it turned where it lay into a long, narrow mountain out in the Baltic Sea. Don't you?"

He paused for a reply, and the other nodded to him. "Go on, so I may hear what you are driving at," said he.

"And mark now, Eric, that this very Öland, where you and I live, is nothing else than the old butterfly-body. If one only stops to think one can see that the island is a butterfly. Toward the north, the slender fore-body and the round head can be seen, and toward the south the lower body, which first broadens out and then narrows down to a sharp point."

Here he paused once more and looked rather quizzically at his companion to see how he took this assertion. But the young man kept right on eating and nodded to him to continue.

"As soon as the butterfly had been changed into a limestone rock, many different kinds of seeds of herbs and trees came travelling along with the winds, and wanted to take root on it. It was a long time before anything but sedge could grow there. Then came sheep-sorrel, the rock-rose and the thorn-brush. But even to-day there is not so much that grows on Alvaret that the mountain is well covered, for it is barren here and there. And no one would think of ploughing and sowing up here, where the earth-crust is so thin. But if you will grant that Alvaret and the strongholds around it are made of the butterfly-body, then you may well have the right to ask what that land which lies beneath the strongholds is."

"Yes, it is just that," said he who was eating. "That I should indeed like to know."

"Well, you must remember that Öland has lain in the sea a good many years, and meantime all the things which tumble around with the waves — seaweed and sand and clams — have gathered around it, and have stayed there. Then, too, stone and gravel have fallen down from both the eastern and the western strongholds. In this way the island has acquired wide shores, where grain and flowers and trees can grow.

"Up here, on the hard butterfly-back, only sheep and cows and ponies go about. The only birds that live here are humble lapwings and plover, and there are no buildings except windmills and a few stone huts, where we shepherds crawl in. But down on the coast lie big villages and churches and parishes and fishing hamlets and a whole city."

He looked searchingly at his comrade, who had finished his meal, and was tying up the food-sack. "I wonder where you will end with all this," said he.

"It is only this that I would know," insisted the shepherd, lowering his voice so that he almost whispered the words, and peering into the mist with his small eyes, which appeared to be worn out from spying after all that which does not exist — "Only this: If the peasants who live on the built-up farms below the strongholds, or the fishermen who take the small herring from the sea, or the merchants in Borgholm, or the bathing guests who come here every summer, or the tourists who wander around in Borgholm's old castle ruin, or the sportsmen who come here in the fall to hunt partridges, or the painters who sit here on Alvaret and paint the sheep and windmills — I should like to know if any of them understand that this island has been a butterfly which once flew about with great shimmery wings."

"Surely it must have occurred to some of them," the young shepherd put in, "as they sat at the edge of the stronghold of an evening, and heard the nightingales trill in the groves below them, and looked over Kalmar Sound, that this island could not have come into existence in the same way as the others."

"I want to ask," said the old one, "if no one has felt a desire to give wings to the windmills — so large that they could reach to heaven; so large that they could lift the whole island out of the sea, and let it fly like a butterfly among butterflies."

"It may be possible that there is something in what you say," returned the young man; "for on summer nights when the heavens widen and open over the island, I have sometimes thought that it was as if it wanted to raise itself from the sea, and fly away."

But when the old man had finally got the young man to talk, he didn't listen to him very much. "I should like to know," resumed the old man in a low tone, "if any one can explain why one feels such a sense of longing up here on Alvaret. I have felt it every day of my life; and I think it preys upon each and every one who must go about here. I want to know if no one else has understood that all this wistfulness is due to the fact that the whole island is a butterfly that longs for its wings."

CHAPTER THIRTEEN

LITTLE KARL'S ISLAND

THE STORM

Friday, April eighth.

THE wild geese had spent the night on Öland's northern point, and were now on their way to the continent. A strong south wind blew over Kalmar Sound, and they had been swept northward. Still they worked their way toward land with good speed. But when they were nearing the first islands a powerful rumbling was heard, as if throngs of strong-winged birds were approaching; and all at once the water under them became perfectly black. Akka drew in her wings so suddenly that she almost stood still in the air. Thereupon, she sank down to light on the surface of the sea. But before the geese reached the water, the storm had caught up with them. It drove before it fogs, salt scum, and small birds; it also caught the wild geese, threw them on end, and cast them out to sea.

It was a rough storm. The wild geese tried time and again to turn back, but couldn't do it, instead they were driven farther and farther out. The storm had already blown them past Öland, and the sea lay before them — empty and desolate. There was nothing for them to do but keep out of the water.

When Akka observed that they were unable to turn back, she thought it needless to let the storm drive them over the

"SEALS! SEALS! SEALS!" CRIED AKKA

entire Baltic. Therefore she sank down to the water. Now the sea was raging, and increasing in violence every second. The sea-green billows rolled forward with seething foam on their crests. Each surged higher than the last. It was as if they raced with each other to see which could foam the wildest. But the wild geese were not afraid of the swells. On the contrary, these seemed to afford them much pleasure. They did not strain themselves swimming, but lay and let themselves be washed up with the swells and down in the water-dales, and had just as much fun as children in a swing. Their only anxiety was that the flock might be separated. The few land-birds who drove by, up in the storm, cried with envy: "There is no danger for you who can swim."

But the wild geese were certainly not out of all danger. In the first place, the rocking made them helplessly sleepy. Time and again they wanted to turn their heads, poke their bills under their wings, and go to sleep. Nothing can be more dangerous than to fall asleep in that way; and Akka kept calling out all the while: "Don't go to sleep, wild geese! He that falls asleep will get away from the flock. He that gets away from the flock is lost."

Despite all attempts at resistance one after another fell asleep; and Akka herself came pretty near dozing off, when she suddenly saw something round and dark rise to the top of a wave. "Seals! Seals! Seals!" cried Akka in a high, shrill voice, and rose into the air with resounding wing-strokes. It was just at the crucial moment. Before the last wild goose had time to come up from the water, the seals were so close to her that they made a grab for her feet.

Then the wild geese were once more up in the storm which drove them before it out to sea. No rest did it allow either itself or the wild geese; and no land did they sight — only desolate sea.

They lit on the water again, as soon as they dared venture. But after rocking upon the waves for a while, they grew sleepy again. And when they fell asleep, the seals came swimming. If old Akka had not been so wakeful, not one of the geese would have escaped.

All day the storm raged; and it caused fearful havoc among the crowds of little birds, which at this time of year were migrating. Some were driven from their course to foreign lands, where they died of starvation; others became so exhausted that they sank down to the sea and were drowned. Many were crushed against the cliff-walls, and many became a prey to the seals.

The storm continued all day, and, at last, Akka began to wonder if she and her flock would perish. They were now dead tired, and nowhere did they see any place where they might rest. At the approach of evening she no longer dared lie down on the sea, for now it filled up all of a sudden with large ice-cakes, which struck against each other, and she feared they would be crushed between the floes. A couple of times the wild geese tried to stand on the ice-crust; but the first time the wild storm swept them into the water; the second time, the merciless seals came creeping up on the ice.

At sundown the wild geese were once more up in the air. They flew on — fearful of the night. The darkness seemed to come upon them much too quickly this night — which was so full of danger.

It was terrible. As yet they could see no land. How would it go with them if they were forced to stay out on the sea all night? They would either be crushed between ice-floes or devoured by seals, or else separated by the storm.

The heavens were cloud-bedecked, the moon hid itself, and the darkness came suddenly. At the same time all nature was filled with a horror which caused the most courageous hearts to quail. Distressed bird-travellers' cries had sounded over the sea all day long without any one having paid the slightest attention to them; but now, when those who uttered them were no longer seen, they seemed mournful and terrifying. Down on the sea, the ice-drifts crashed against each other with a loud rumbling noise. The seals tuned up their wild hunting songs. It was as though heaven and earth were about to clash.

THE SHEEP

THE boy sat for a moment looking down into the sea. Suddenly he thought it began to roar louder than ever. He glanced up. Right in front of him — only a couple of metres away — loomed a rugged and bare mountain-wall. At its base the waves dashed into a foam-like spray. The wild geese flew straight toward the cliff, and the boy did not see how they could avoid being dashed to pieces against it. No sooner had he wondered that Akka hadn't seen the danger in time than they were over by the mountain. Then he also noticed that before them was the arched entrance to a grotto, into which the geese steered. The next moment they were safe.

The first thing the wild geese thought of — before they gave themselves time to rejoice over their safety — was to see if all their comrades were also harboured. Yes, there were Akka, Iksi, Kolmi, Neljä, Viisi, Kuusi, all the six goslings, the goosey-gander, Dunfin and Thumbietot; but Kaksi from Nuolja, the first left-hand goose, was missing — and none knew anything about her fate.

When the wild geese discovered that no one but Kaksi had been separated from the flock, they took the matter lightly. Kaksi was old and wise. She knew all their ways and habits, and she, of course, would know how to find her way back to them.

Now the geese began to look around in the cave. Enough daylight came in through the opening so that they could see the grotto was both deep and wide. They were congratulating themselves on having found such a fine night harbour, when one of the flock caught sight of some shining, green dots, that glittered in a dark corner. "Those are eyes!" cried Akka. "There are big animals in here." They rushed toward the opening, but Thumbietot called to them: "There is nothing to run away from! It's only a few sheep lying alongside the grotto wall."

When the wild geese had accustomed themselves to the dim daylight in the cave, they could see the sheep very distinctly. The grown-up sheep might be about as many as there were geese; but beside these there were a few little lambs. An old ram, with long, twisted horns, appeared to be the most lordly one of the flock. The wild geese stepped up to him with much bowing and scraping. "Well met in the wilderness!" they greeted, but the big ram lay still, and did not speak a word of welcome.

Then the wild geese thought that the sheep were displeased because they had taken shelter in their grotto. "Our coming here is not agreeable perhaps?" said Akka. "But we cannot help it, for we are wind-driven. We have wandered about in the storm all day, and it would be very good to be allowed to stop here to-night." After that there was a long pause before any of the sheep answered with words; but, on the other hand, it could be heard distinctly that one or two of them heaved deep sighs. Akka knew, to be sure, that sheep are always shy and peculiar; but these seemed to have no idea as to how they should conduct themselves. Finally an old ewe, who had a long and pathetic face and a doleful voice, said: "There isn't one among us that would refuse to let you stay; but this is a house of mourning, and we cannot receive guests, as in former days." "You needn't let that worry you," said Akka. "If you knew what we have endured this day, you would surely understand that we are satisfied if we only get a safe spot to sleep on."

When Akka said that, the old ewe raised herself. "I believe it would be better for you to fly about in the worst kind of storm than to stop here. But, at least you shall not go from here before we have had the privilege of offering you the best hospitality which the house affords."

She conducted them to a hollow in the ground, which was filled with water. Beside it lay a pile of bait and husks and chaff; and she bade them make the most of these. "This year we have had a severe snow-winter on the island," said she. "The peasants who own us came out to us with hay and oaten straw, so we shouldn't starve to death. And this trash is all there is left of the good cheer."

The geese promptly made a rush for the food. They thought they had fared well, and were in their best humour. They must have observed, however, that the sheep were anxious; but they knew how easily scared sheep always are, and didn't believe there was any actual danger on foot. As soon as they had eaten, they meant to stand up to sleep as usual. But presently the big ram got up and walked over to them. The geese thought they had never seen a sheep with such big and coarse horns. In other respects, also, he was noticeable. He had a high, rolling forehead, intelligent eyes, and a good bearing — as if he were a proud and courageous animal.

"I cannot assume the responsibility of letting you geese remain, without telling you that it is unsafe here," he said. "We cannot receive night guests just now." At last Akka began to comprehend that this was serious. "We will go away, since you really wish it," said she. "But won't you tell us first, what it is that troubles you? We know nothing about it. We do not even know where we are." "This is Little Karl's Island!" said the ram. "It lies outside of Gottland, and only sheep and sea-birds live here." "Perhaps you are wild sheep?" said Akka. "We're not far removed from it," replied the ram. "We have nothing to do with human beings. It's an old agreement between us and some peasants on a farm in Gottland, that they shall supply us with fodder in case we have snow-winter; and as a recompense they are permitted to take away those of us who become superfluous. The island is small, so it cannot feed very many of us. But otherwise we take care of ourselves all the year around, and we do not live in houses with doors and locks, but in grottoes like these."

"Do you stay out here in the winter as well?" asked Akka, surprised. "We do," answered the ram. "We have good fodder up here on the mountain throughout the year." "It sounds as if you were better off than other sheep," said Akka. "But what is the misfortune that has befallen you?" "It was bitter cold last winter. The sea froze, and then three foxes came over the ice, and here they have been ever since. Otherwise, there are no dangerous animals on the island." "Oho! do foxes dare to attack such as you?" "Oh, no! not during the day, when I can protect myself and mine," said the ram, shaking his horns. "But they sneak upon us at night when we sleep in the grottoes. We try to keep awake, but one must sleep some of the time; and then they come upon us. They have already killed every sheep in the other grottoes, and there were herds that were just as large as mine."

"It isn't pleasant to tell that we are so helpless," said the old ewe. "We cannot defend ourselves any better than if we were tame sheep." "Do you think that they will come here to-night?" asked Akka. "There is nothing else in store for us," answered the old ewe. "They were here last night, and stole a lamb from us. They'll be sure to come back, as long as there are any of us alive. That is what they have done in the other places." "But if they are allowed to keep this up, you'll become entirely extinct," said Akka. "Oh! it won't be long before it's all over with the sheep on Little Karl's Island," sighed the ewe.

Akka stood there hesitatingly. It was by no means a pleasant prospect to venture out in the storm again, nor was it well to remain in a house where such guests were expected. When she had pondered a while, she turned to Thumbietot. "I wonder if you will help us, as you have done so many times before," said she. Yes, that he would love to do, he replied. "It is a pity for you not to get any sleep!" said the wild goose, "but I wonder if you are able to keep awake until the foxes come, and then to awaken us, so we may fly away." The boy was not very glad of this; but anything was better than going out in the storm again — so he promised to keep awake.

He went over to the grotto opening, crawled in behind a

stone that he might be sheltered from the storm, and sat down to watch.

When the boy had been sitting there a while, the storm abated, the sky grew clear and the moonlight began to play on the waves. The boy stepped to the opening to look out. The grotto was rather high up on the mountain. A narrow and steep path led to it. It was probably here that he must await the foxes.

As yet he saw no foxes; but, on the other hand, there was something which, for the moment, terrified him much more. On the land-strip below the mountain stood some giants, or other stone-trolls — or perhaps they were actual human beings. He thought at first that he was dreaming, but now he was positive that he had not fallen asleep. He saw the big men so distinctly that it could be no illusion. Some stood on the land-strip, others right on the mountain-wall as if about to climb it. Some had big, thick heads; others had no heads at all. Some were one-armed, and some had humps both before and behind. He had never seen anything so extraordinary.

The boy stood there and worked himself into a state of panic because of those trolls, and he almost forgot to keep his eye peeled for the foxes. But now he heard the scraping of claws and saw three foxes coming up the steep. As soon as he knew that he had something real to deal with, he was calm again, and not the least bit scared. It occurred to him that it would be a pity to awaken only the geese, and leave the sheep to their fate. He thought he would like to arrange things some other way.

He ran quickly to the other end of the grotto, shook the big ram's horns until he awoke, and at the same time swung himself upon his back. "Get up, daddy, and we'll try to frighten the foxes a bit!" said the boy.

He had tried to be as quiet as possible, but the foxes must have heard some noise; for when they came up to the mouth of the grotto they stopped and deliberated. "It was certainly some one in there that moved," said one. "I wonder if they are awake." "Just you go ahead!" said another. "At all events, they can't do anything to us."

When they came farther into the grotto, they stopped and sniffed. "Whom shall we take to-night?" whispered the one in the lead. "To-night we will take the big ram," said the last. "After that, we'll have easy work with the rest."

The boy sat on the old ram's back and saw how they sneaked along. "Now butt straight ahead!" whispered the boy. The ram butted, and the first fox was thrust — top over tail — back to the opening. "Now butt to the left!" said the boy, turning the big ram's head in that direction. The ram measured a terrific assault that caught the second fox in the side. He rolled over several times before he got to his feet again and made his escape. The boy had wished that the third one, too, might have got a bump, but this one had already skedaddled.

"Now I think that they've had enough for to-night," said the boy. "So do I," agreed the big ram. "Now lie down on my back, and creep into the wool! You deserve to have it warm and comfortable, after all the wind and storm that you have been out in."

HELL'S HOLE

THE next day the big ram went around with the boy on his back, and showed him the island. It consisted of a single massive mountain. It was like a large house with perpendicular walls and a flat roof. First the ram walked up on the mountain roof and showed the boy the good grazing lands there; and he had to admit that the island seemed to be especially created for sheep. There wasn't much else than sheep-sorrel and such little spicy growths as sheep are fond of that grew on the mountain.

But indeed there was something beside sheep-fodder to look at, for one who was well up on the cliff. To begin with, the large expanse of sea — which now lay blue and sunlit, and rolled forward in glittering swells — was visible. Only upon one and another point did the foam spray up. To the east lay Gottland, with its even and long-stretched coast; and to the southwest lay Great Karl's Island, which was built on the same plan as the little island. When the ram walked to the very edge of the mountain roof, so the boy could look down the mountain walls, he noticed that they were simply filled with birds' nests; and in the blue sea beneath lay surf-scoters and eider-ducks and kittiwakes and guillemots and razor-bills — so pretty and peaceful — busying themselves with fishing for small herring.

"This is really a favoured land," said the boy. "You live in a pretty place, you sheep." "Oh, yes! it's pretty enough here," said the big ram. It was as if he wished to add something; but he didn't, he only sighed. "If you go about here alone you must watch out for the crevices which run all around the mountain," he cautioned after a pause. And this was a good warning, for there were deep and broad crevices in several places. The largest of them was called Hell's Hole. That crevice was many fathoms deep and nearly six feet wide. "If one were to fall down there, it would certainly be the last of him," said the big ram. The boy thought it sounded as if he had a special meaning in what he said.

Then he conducted the boy down to the narrow strip of shore. Now he could see those giants that had frightened him the night before, at close range. They were nothing but tall rock-pillars. The big ram called them "boulders." The boy couldn't see enough of them. He thought that if there had ever been any trolls who had turned into stone they ought to look just like that.

Although it was pretty down on the shore, the boy liked it even better on the mountain height. It was ghastly down here; for everywhere they came across dead sheep. It was here that the foxes held their orgies. He saw skeletons whose flesh had been eaten, and bodies that were half-eaten, and others that they had scarcely tasted. It was heart-rending to see how the wild beasts had thrown themselves upon the sheep just for sport — only to hunt them and tear them to death.

The big ram did not pause in front of the dead, but walked by them in silence. But the boy, meanwhile, could not help seeing all the horror.

Then the big ram started up the mountain again. When he was there he stopped and said: "If some one who is capable and wise could see all the misery which prevails here he surely would not be able to rest until these foxes had been punished." "The foxes must live, too," said the boy. "Yes," admitted the big ram, "those who do not tear in pieces more animals than they need for their sustenance, they may as well live. But these are felons." "The peasants who own the island ought to come here and help you," declared the boy. "They have rowed over a number of times," replied the ram, "but the foxes always hid themselves in the grottoes and crevices, so they could not shoot at them." "You surely cannot mean, daddy, that a poor little creature like me should be able to get at them, when neither you nor the peasants have succeeded in getting the better of them." "One that is little and spry, can put many things to rights," said the big ram.

They talked no more about this, and the boy went over and sat down among the wild geese, who were feeding on the highland. Although he had not cared to show his feelings before the ram, he was very sad on the sheep's account, and he would have been glad to help them. "I can at least talk with Akka and Morten Goosey-gander about the matter," thought he. "Perhaps they can help me with a good suggestion."

A little later the white goosey-gander took the boy on his back and crossed the mountain plain, in the direction of Hell's Hole at that!

He wandered, carefree, on the broad mountain roof — apparently unconscious of how large and white he was. He didn't seek protection behind tufts, or any other protuberances, but went straight ahead. It was singular that he was not more careful, for it was obvious that he had fared badly in yesterday's storm. He limped on his right leg, and his left wing hung and dragged as if it were broken.

He acted as if there were no danger, pecked at a grassblade here and another there, and did not look about him in any direction. The boy lay stretched out full length on the goose-back, and looked up toward the blue sky. He was so accustomed to riding now that he could both stand up and lie down on the goose-back.

While the goosey-gander and the boy were so carefree,

they did not observe, of course, that the three foxes had come up on the mountain plain.

And the foxes, who knew that it was well-nigh impossible to take the life of a goose on an open plain, thought at first that they wouldn't chase after the goosey-gander. But since they had nothing else to do, they finally sneaked down into one of the long cracks, and tried to steal up to him. They went about it so cautiously that the goosey-gander couldn't see a shadow of them.

They were not far off when the goosey-gander made an attempt to raise himself into the air. He spread his wings, but he did not manage to lift himself. When the foxes seemed to grasp the fact that he couldn't fly, they hurried forward with greater eagerness than before. They no longer concealed themselves in the cleft, but came out on the highland. They hurried as fast as they could, behind tufts and hollows, coming nearer and nearer to the goosey-gander — without his seeming to notice that he was being hunted. At last the foxes were so near that they could make the final leap. Simultaneously, all three threw themselves with one long jump at the goosey-gander.

But yet at the last moment he must have noticed something, for he ran out of the way, and the foxes missed him. This, at any rate, didn't mean very much, for the goosey-gander only had a couple of metres headway, and, in the bargain, he limped. Anyhow, the poor thing ran ahead as fast as he could.

The boy sat upon the goose-back — backward — and shrieked and called to the foxes. "You have eaten yourselves too fat on mutton, foxes. You can't catch up with a goose even." He teased them so that they became crazed with rage and thought only of rushing forward.

The white one ran right straight to the big cleft. When he was there, he made one stroke with his wings and was over. Just then the foxes were almost upon him.

The goosey-gander hurried on with the same haste as before, even after he had got across Hell's Hole. But he had hardly run two metres when the boy patted him on the neck, and said: "Now you can stop, goosey-gander."

At that instant they heard wild howls behind them, and a scraping of claws, and heavy falls. But of the foxes they saw nothing more.

The next morning the keeper of the lighthouse on Great Karl's Island found a bit of bark poked under the entrance-door, and on it was carved in slanting, angular letters: "The foxes on the little island have fallen down into Hell's Hole. Take care of them!"

And this the keeper of the lighthouse did, too.

CHAPTER FOURTEEN

TWO CITIES

THE CITY AT THE BOTTOM OF THE SEA

Saturday, April ninth.

IT WAS a calm and clear night. The wild geese did not bother to seek shelter in any of the grottoes, but stood and slept on the mountain top; and the boy had lain down in the short, dry grass beside the geese.

It was bright moonlight that night; so bright that it was difficult for the boy to go to sleep. He lay there wondering how long he had been away from home and figured out that it was three weeks since he had started on the trip. At the same time he remembered that this was Easter-eve.

"It is to-night that all the witches come home from Blåkulla," thought he, laughing to himself. For he was just a little afraid of both the water-sprite and the elf, but he didn't believe the least little bit in witches.

If there had been any witches out that night, he should have seen them, to be sure. It was so light in the heavens that not the tiniest black speck could move in the air without his seeing it.

As the boy lay there with his nose in the air thinking about this, he caught sight of something lovely! The moon's disc was whole and round, and rather high, and over it a big bird came flying. It did not fly past the moon, but moved as if it might have flown out from it. The bird looked black against the light background, and the wings extended from one rim of the disc to the other. It flew on evenly, in the same direction, and the boy thought that it was painted on the moon. The body was small, the neck long and slender, the legs hung down, long and thin. It couldn't be anything but a stork.

A couple of seconds later Herr Ermenrich, the stork, lit beside the boy. He bent down and poked him with his bill, to awaken him.

Instantly the boy sat up. "I'm not asleep, Herr Ermenrich," he said. "How does it happen that you are out in the middle of the night, and how is everything at Glimminge Castle? Do you want to speak with Mother Akka?"

"It's too light to sleep to-night," answered Herr Ermenrich. "Therefore I decided to fly over here to Karl's Island to hunt you up, friend Thumbietot. I learned from the seamew that you were spending the night here. I have not as yet moved over to Glimminge Castle, but am still living at Pommern."

The boy was simply overjoyed to think that Herr Ermenrich had sought him out. They chatted about all sorts of things, like old friends. At last the stork asked the boy if he wouldn't like to go out riding for a while on this beautiful night.

Oh, yes! that the boy wanted to do, if the stork would manage to get him back to the wild geese before sunrise. This he promised, so off they went.

Again Herr Ermenrich flew straight toward the moon. They rose and rose; the sea sank deep down, but the flight went so light and easy that to the boy it seemed almost as if he were lying still in the air.

When Herr Ermenrich began to descend, the boy thought that the flight had lasted an unreasonably short time.

They landed on a desolate bit of seashore that was covered with fine, even sand. All along the coast ran a row of sand-dunes with lyme-grass on their tops. They were not very high, but they prevented the boy from seeing any of the island.

Herr Ermenrich stood on a dune, drew up one leg, and bent his head backward, so he could stick his bill under his wing. "You can roam around on the shore for a while," he said to Thumbietot, "while I rest myself. But don't go so far away that you can't find your way back to me!"

To start with, the boy intended to climb a sand-dune to see how the land behind it looked. But when he had gone a couple of paces, he stubbed the toe of his wooden shoe against something hard. He stooped down, and saw a small copper coin lying on the sand. The coin was so worn with verdigris that it was almost transparent; and so poor that he didn't even bother to pick it up, but only kicked it out of the way.

When he straightened up he was perfectly astounded, for two paces away from him stood a high, dark wall with a big, turreted gate.

The moment before the boy had bent down, the sea lay there — shimmering and smooth, while now it was hidden by a long wall with towers and battlements. Directly in front of him, where before there had been only a few seaweed banks, the big gate of the wall opened.

The boy probably understood that it was a spectre-play of some sort; so this was nothing to be afraid of, thought he. It wasn't any dangerous witch or troll, or any other evil — such as he always dreaded to encounter at night. Both the wall and the gate were so beautifully constructed that his only desire was to see what there might be back of them. "I must find out what this is," he thought, and went in through the gate.

In the deep archway were guards, dressed in brocaded and puffed suits, their long-handled spears beside them — who sat and threw dice. They thought only of the game, and took no notice of the boy who hurried past them.

Just within the gate he found an open space, paved with large, even stones. Round about were rows of high and magnificent buildings, between which opened long, narrow streets. On the square — facing the gate — it fairly swarmed with human beings. The men wore long, fur-trimmed capes over satin suits; plume-bedecked hats sat obliquely on their heads; on their chests hung superb chains. They were all so regally attired that the whole lot of them might have been kings.

The women went about in high headdresses and long robes with tight-fitting sleeves. They, too, were beautifully dressed, but their splendour was not to be compared with that of the men.

This was exactly like the old story-book, which mother took from the chest — only once — and showed to him. The boy simply couldn't believe his eyes.

But that which was even more wonderful to look at than the men or the women, was the city itself. Every house was built with a gable that faced the street. And the gables were so highly ornamented that one would think they were trying to compete with each other as to which could show the most beautiful decorations.

When suddenly seeing so much that is new, one cannot manage to treasure it all in one's memory. But at least the boy could recall having seen stairway gables on the various landings which bore images of the Christ and his Apostles; gables where there were images in niche after niche all along the wall; gables that were inlaid with multi-coloured bits of glass, and gables that were striped and checked in white and black marble. As the boy was admiring all this, a sudden sense of haste came over him. "Anything like this my eyes have never seen before. Anything like this they would never see again," he said to himself. And he ran into the city — up one street, and down another.

The streets were straight and narrow, but not empty and gloomy, as they were in the cities with which he was familiar. There were people everywhere. Old women sat by their open doors and spun without a spinning-wheel — only with the help of a shuttle. The merchants' shops were like market-stalls — opening onto the street. All the handicraftsmen did their work out of doors. In one place they were boiling crude oil; in another tanning hides; in a third there was a long rope-walk.

If only the boy had had time enough he could have learned how to make all sorts of things. Here he saw how armourers hammered out thin breast-plates; how jewellers set precious stones in rings and bracelets; how turners tended their irons; how the shoemakers soled soft, red shoes; how the gold-wire drawers twisted gold thread, and how the weavers inserted silver and gold into their cloth.

But the boy did not have time to stay. He only rushed on, that he might see as much as possible before all would vanish again.

The high wall ran clear round the city and fenced it in, as a hedge shuts in a field. He saw it at the end of every street — gable ornamented and crenulated. On top of the wall walked warriors in shining armour; and when he had run from one end of the city to the other, he came to still another gate in the wall. Beyond this wall lay the sea and harbour. The boy saw olden-time ships, with rowing-benches straight across, and high structures fore and aft. Some lay and took on cargo, others were just casting anchor. Carriers and merchants hurried past each other. All over there was life and bustle.

But not even here did he have the time to linger. He rushed into the city again; and now he came up to the big square. There stood the cathedral with its three high towers and deep vaulted arches filled with images. Its walls had been so richly decorated by sculptors that there was not a stone without its own special ornamentation. And what a magnificent display of gilded crosses, and gold-trimmed altars, and priests in golden vestments shimmered through the open gate! Directly opposite the church there was a house with a notched roof and a single, slender, sky-high tower. That was probably the courthouse. And between the courthouse and the cathedral, all around the square, stood the beautiful gabled houses, with their multiplicity of adornments.

The boy had run himself both warm and tired. He thought that now he had seen the most remarkable things, and therefore he began to walk more leisurely. The street into which he now turned was surely the one where the inhabitants purchased their fine clothing. He saw crowds of people standing before the little stalls where the merchants spread brocades, stiff satins, heavy gold cloth, shimmery velvet, delicate veiling, and laces as sheer as a spider's web.

Before, when the boy ran so fast, no one paid any attention to him. The people must have thought it was only a little gray rat that darted by them. But now, as he walked down the street, very leisurely, one of the salesmen caught sight of him, and began to beckon to him.

At first the boy was uneasy and wanted to hurry out of the way, but the salesman only beckoned and smiled, and spread out on the counter a lovely piece of satin damask, as if to tempt him.

The boy shook his head. "I will never be so rich that I can buy even a yard of that cloth," thought he.

But now they had caught sight of him in every stall, all along the street. Wherever he looked stood a salesman beckoning to him. They left their costly wares, and thought only of him. He saw how they hurried into the most hidden corner of the stall to fetch the best they had to sell, and how their hands trembled with eagerness and haste as they laid it upon the counter.

When the boy kept on going, one of the merchants jumped over the counter, caught hold of him, and spread before him silver cloth and woven tapestries, which shone in brilliant colours.

The boy could only laugh at him. The salesman must surely understand that a poor little creature like him couldn't buy such things. He stood still and held out his two empty hands so they would understand that he had nothing, and let him go in peace.

But the merchant raised a finger and nodded and pushed the whole pile of beautiful things over to him.

"Can he mean that he will sell all this for a gold piece?" wondered the boy.

The merchant brought out a tiny worn and poor coin—

the smallest there was — and showed it to him. And he was so eager to sell that he increased his pile with a pair of large, heavy, silver goblets.

Then the boy began to dig down in his pockets. He knew, of course, that he didn't possess a single coin, but he couldn't help feeling for it.

All the other merchants stood by to see how the sale would come off, and when they observed that the boy began to search in his pockets, they flung themselves over the counters, took up handfuls of gold and silver ornaments, and offered them to him. And they all showed him that what they asked in payment was just one little penny.

The boy turned both vest and breeches pockets inside out, so they should see that he owned nothing. Then tears filled the eyes of all these regal merchants, who were so much richer than he. At last he was moved because they looked so distressed and pondered if he could not in some way help them. And then he happened to think of the rusty coin, which he had but lately seen on the strand.

He started to run down the street, and luck was with him, so that he came to the self-same gate that he had happened upon first. He dashed through it, and commenced to search for the little green copper penny that lay on the strand a while ago.

He found it, too, very promptly; but when he had picked it up, and wanted to run back to the city with it — he saw only the sea before him. No city wall, no gate, no sentinels, no streets, no houses were now visible — only the sea.

The boy couldn't help that the tears came to his eyes. He had believed, in the beginning, that that which he had seen was only an illusion; but this he had already forgotten. He only thought how beautiful it all was.

He felt a genuine, deep sorrow because the city had vanished.

That moment Herr Ermenrich awoke, and came up to him. But he didn't hear him, and the stork had to poke the boy with his bill to attract attention to himself. "I believe that you stand here and sleep the way I do," said Herr Ermenrich.

"Oh, Herr Ermenrich!" the boy exclaimed. "What was that city which stood here just now?"

"Have you seen a city?" questioned the stork. "You have slept and dreamt I say."

"No! I have not dreamt," said Thumbietot, and he told the stork all that he had experienced.

Then Herr Ermenrich said: "For my part, Thumbietot, I believe that you fell asleep here on the strand and dreamed all this. But I will not conceal from you that Bataki, the raven, who is the most learned of all birds, once told me that in former times there was a city on this shore, called Vineta. It was so rich and so fortunate that no city has ever been more glorious; but its inhabitants, unluckily, gave themselves up to arrogance and love of display. As a punishment, says Bataki, the city of Vineta was overtaken by a flood, and sank into the sea. But these inhabitants cannot die, nor is their city destroyed. And one night in every hundred years, it rises in all its splendour up from the sea, and remains on the surface just one hour."

"Yes; it must be so," said Thumbietot, "for this I have seen."

"But when the hour is up, it sinks again into the sea, if, during that time, no merchant in Vineta has sold anything to a single living creature. If you, Thumbietot, had only had ever so tiny a coin to pay the merchants, Vineta might have remained up here on the shore; and its people could have lived and died like other human beings."

"Herr Ermenrich," said the boy, "now I understand why you came and fetched me in the middle of the night. It was because you believed that I should be able to save the old city. I am so sorry it didn't turn out as you wished, Herr Ermenrich."

He covered his face with his hands and wept. It was hard to tell which looked the more disconsolate — the boy or Herr Ermenrich.

THE LIVING CITY

Monday, April eleventh.

On Easter Monday, the wild geese and Thumbietot were on the wing. They travelled over Gottland.

The large island lay smooth and even below them. The ground was checked just as in Skåne, and there were many churches and farms.

The wild geese had taken the route over Gottland on account of Thumbietot. He had not been himself for two days, and had not spoken a cheerful word. This was because he had thought of nothing but that city which had appeared to him in such a strange way. He had never seen anything so beautiful and he could not be reconciled with himself for having failed to save it. He was not usually soft-hearted, but now he actually mourned for the beautiful buildings and the stately people.

Both Akka and the goosey-gander had tried to convince Thumbietot that he was the victim of a dream or an illusion, but the boy wouldn't listen to anything of the sort. He was so positive that he had really seen what he had seen that no one could move him in his conviction. He went about so disconsolate that his travelling companions became uneasy for him.

Just as the boy was most depressed, old Kaksi came back to the flock. She had been blown toward Gottland, and compelled to travel over the whole island before she learned from some crows that her comrades were on Little Karl's Island. When Kaksi found out what was wrong with Thumbietot, she said impulsivly:

"If Thumbietot is grieving over an old city, we'll soon be able to comfort him. Come along, and I'll take you to a place that I saw yesterday! He'll get over his distress before long."

The geese were soon on their way to the place which Kaksi wished to show Thumbietot. Blue as he was, he couldn't keep from looking down at the land over which he travelled, as usual.

He thought it looked as if the whole island had in the beginning been just such a high, steep cliff as Karl's Island — though much bigger of course. But afterward, it had in some way been flattened out. Some one must have rolled a big rolling-pin over it, as if it had been a lump of dough. Not that the island had become altogether flat and even, like a bread-cake, for it wasn't like that. While travelling alongside the coast, he had seen, here and there, white lime walls with grottoes and crags but in most places the ground was level, and the shores sank modestly down toward the sea.

In Gottland they had a pleasant and peaceful holiday afternoon. It turned out to be mild spring weather; the trees had big buds; spring blossoms dressed the ground in the leafy meadows; the poplars' long, thin pendants swayed;

and in the little gardens, which are to be found around every cottage, the gooseberry bushes were green.

The warmth and the budding of spring had tempted the people out into gardens and roads, and wherever a number of them had come together, they played games. Not only the children played but the grown-ups also. They threw stones at a given point, and they sent balls so high into the air that they almost touched the wild geese. It looked cheerful and pleasant to see big folks at play; and the boy certainly would have enjoyed it had he only been able to forget his grief and disappointment because of his failure to save the ancient city.

But anyhow, he had to admit that this was a lovely trip. The air was so full of joy and melody. Little children played ring games, and sang as they played. The Salvation Army was out. He saw a lot of people dressed in black and red sitting upon a wooded hill, playing on guitars and brass instruments. Down a road came a great crowd of people. They were Good Templars who had been on a pleasure trip. He recognized them by the big banners, with the gold inscriptions, which waved above them. They sang song after song as long as he could hear them.

After that the boy could never think of Gottland without thinking of the games and songs at the same time.

He had been sitting, looking down a long while, when he happened to raise his eyes. His amazement was indescribable. Before he was aware of it, the wild geese had left the interior of the island and gone westward — toward the seacoast. Now the wide, blue sea lay before him. However, it was not the sea that was remarkable, but a city which appeared on the shore.

The boy was coming from the east, and the sun had just begun to sink in the west. As he drew nearer the city, its walls and towers and high, gabled houses and churches stood there quite black against the light evening sky. Therefore, he couldn't see what it was really like, and for a moment or two he believed that this city was just as beautiful as the one he had seen on Easter-eve.

When he came right up to it, he saw that it was both like and unlike that city from the bottom of the sea. There was the same contrast between these two cities as there is between a man whom one sees arrayed in purple and jewels one day, and another day dressed in rags.

Yes, once upon a time, this city had probably been like the one of which he sat dreaming. This one was also enclosed by a wall with towers and gates. But the towers in this city, which had been allowed to remain on land, were roofless, hollow, and empty. The gates were without doors; sentinels and warriors had disappeared. All the glittering splendour was past and gone. There was nothing left but the naked, gray stone skeleton.

As the boy came farther into the city, he saw that the larger part of it was made up of small, low houses; but here and there stood a few high gabled houses and cathedrals which were from the olden time. The walls of the gabled houses were painted white, and entirely without ornamentation; but because the boy had so lately seen the buried city, he seemed to understand how they once had been decorated: some with statues, and others with black and white marble. And it was the same with the old cathedrals; they were mostly roofless with bare interiors. The window openings were empty, the floors grass-grown, and ivy clambered along the walls. But now he knew how they had looked once upon a time: they had been covered with paintings and images; the chancel had been adorned with altars and gilded crosses, and there priests had moved, arrayed in golden vestments.

The boy saw also the narrow streets, which were almost deserted on this holiday afternoon. He knew, he did, what throngs of stately people had once upon a time swarmed there!

But that which Nils Holgersson did not see was, that the city even to-day is both beautiful and quaint. He saw neither the cozy cottages on the side streets, with their white-trimmed black walls, the red geraniums behind the shining window-panes, nor the many pretty gardens and avenues, nor the beauty of the vine-clad ruins. His mind was so filled with the preceding splendour that he could see no beauty in the present.

The wild geese flew back and forth over the city several times, so that Thumbietot might see everything. Finally, they sank down on the grass-grown floor of a cathedral ruin, to spend the night.

Long after they had gone to sleep, Thumbietot was still awake and sat gazing up through the open arches at the evening sky. When he had sat there a while, he made up his mind not to grieve any more because he hadn't been able to save the buried city.

No, that he shouldn't do, now that he had seen this one. If the other city had not sunk into the sea again, then perhaps in time it would have become as dilapidated as this one. Perhaps it could not have resisted time and decay, but would have stood there with roofless churches and bare houses and desolate, empty streets — just like this one. Then it was better that it should remain in all its glory down in the deep.

"What happened was best," thought he. "If I had the power to save the city, I don't believe that I should care to do it." Then he no longer grieved over that matter.

And there are doubtless many among the younger generation who think in the same way. But when people are old, and have accustomed themselves to being satisfied with little, then they are more happy over the Visby that lives, than over a magnificent Vineta at the bottom of the sea.

CHAPTER FIFTEEN

THE LEGEND OF SMÅLAND

Tuesday, April twelfth.

THE wild geese had made a good trip over the sea, and had alighted in Tjust Parish in northern Småland. That parish seemed unable to make up its mind whether it wanted to be land or sea. Bays ran in everywhere, and cut the land up into islands and peninsulas and points and capes. The sea was so forceful that the only things which could hold themselves above it were hills and mountains. All the lowlands were hidden away, under the water.

It was evening when the wild geese came in from the sea; and the land with the little hills lay prettily between the shimmering bays. Here and there, on the islands, the boy saw cabins and cottages; and the farther inland he travelled, the bigger and better became the dwelling houses, till, finally, they grew into large, white manors. Along the shores was a border of trees; and beyond lay field-plots, and on the tops of the little hills there were more trees. He could not help but think of Blekinge. Here again was a place where land and sea met in a charming and peaceful way, trying, as it were, to show each other the best and loveliest they possessed.

The wild geese alighted upon a barren rock island in Goose Bay. The first glance at the shore assured them that spring had made rapid strides while they were on the islands. The big, fine trees were not as yet leaf-clad, but the ground under them was brocaded with white anemones, gagea, and blue anemones.

When the wild geese saw the flower-carpet they feared that they had lingered too long in the southern part of the country. Akka immediately remarked that there was no time in which to look up any of the stopping places in Småland. By the next morning they must travel northward, over Östergotland.

The boy should then see nothing of Småland, which grieved him. He had heard more about Småland than about any other province, and he had longed to see it with his own eyes.

The summer before, when he served as goose-boy with a farmer in the neighbourhood of Jordberga, he used to meet almost every day two Småland children, who also tended geese. These children had irritated him terribly with their Småland.

It wouldn't be fair to say that Osa, the goose-girl, had annoyed him. She was much too wise for that. But the one who could be aggravating with a vengeance was her brother, little Mats.

"Have you heard, Nils Goose-boy, what happened when Småland and Skåne were created?" he would ask, and if Nils Holgersson said no, he promptly began to relate the old joke-legend.

"Well, it happened at the time when Our Lord was creating the world. While he was doing his best work, Saint Peter came along. He stopped and looked on, and then he asked if it was hard work. 'Well, it isn't exactly easy,' said Our Lord. Saint Peter stood there a while longer, and when he noticed how easy it appeared to lay out one landscape after another, he too wanted to try his hand at it. 'Perhaps you need to rest yourself a little,' said Saint Peter, 'I could attend to the work in the meantime for you.' But this Our Lord did not wish. 'I do not know if you are so much at home in this art that I can trust you to take hold where I leave off,' he answered. Then Saint Peter was angry, and said that he believed he could create just as fine countries as Our Lord himself.

"It so happened that Our Lord was just then creating Småland. It wasn't even half ready but it looked as if it would become an indescribably beautiful and fertile land. It was difficult for Our Lord to say no to Saint Peter, and, besides, he thought very likely that a thing so well begun no one could spoil. Therefore he said: 'If you like, we will prove which of us understands this sort of work the better. You, who are only a novice, shall go on with this, which I have begun, and I will create a new land.' To this Saint Peter agreed at once; so they went to work — each in his place.

"Our Lord moved southward a bit, where he undertook to create Skåne. And it wasn't long before he was through with it, and asked if Saint Peter had also finished, and would come to look at his work. 'Mine was ready long ago,' said Saint Peter; and from the sound of his voice it was plain how pleased he was with what he had accomplished.

"When Saint Peter saw Skåne, he had to acknowledge that there was nothing but good to be said of that country. It was a fertile land and easy to cultivate, with wide plains wherever one looked, and with hardly a sign of hills. It was evident that Our Lord had really contemplated making it such that people would feel at home there. 'Yes, this is a good country,' said Saint Peter, 'but I think that mine is better.' 'Then we'll take a look at it,' said Our Lord.

"The land was already finished in the north and east when Saint Peter began the work, but the southern and western parts, and the whole interior, he had created all by himself. Now when Our Lord came up there, where Saint Peter had been at work, he was so horrified that he stopped short and exclaimed: 'What on earth have you been doing to this land, Saint Peter?'

"Saint Peter, too, stood looking around — perfectly astonished. He had had the idea that nothing could be so good for a land as a great deal of heat. Therefore he had gathered together an enormous mass of stones and mountains, and had erected a highland, and this he had done so that it might be near the sun, and receive much help from the sun's heat. Over the stone-heaps he had spread a thin layer of soil, and then he had thought that everything was well arranged.

"But while he was down in Skåne, a couple of heavy showers had come up, and more was not needed to show what his work amounted to. When Our Lord came to inspect the land, all the soil had been washed away, and the naked rock foundation shone forth all over. Where it was about the best, lay clay and heavy gravel over the rocks, but it looked so poor that it was plainly to be seen that little else than spruce and juniper and moss and heather could grow there. But what there was plenty of was water! It covered all the clefts in the mountain; and lakes and rivers and brooks were everywhere, to say nothing of swamps and morasses, which spread over large areas. And the most exasperating of it all was, that while some tracts had too much water, it was so scarce in others that whole fields lay like dry moors, where sand and earth whirled up in clouds with the least little breeze.

"'What can have been your meaning in creating such a land as this?' said Our Lord. Saint Peter made excuses, and declared he had wished to build up a land so high that it should have plenty of warmth from the sun. 'But then you will also get much of the night chill,' said Our Lord, 'for that too comes from heaven. I am very much afraid the little that can grow here will freeze.'

"This to be sure, Saint Peter hadn't thought about.

"'Yes, here it will be a poor and frost-bound land,' said Our Lord. 'It can't be helped.'"

When little Mats had got this far in his story, Osa, the goose-girl, protested: "I cannot bear, little Mats, to hear you say that it is so miserable in Småland. You forget entirely how much good soil there is there. Only think of Möre district, by Kalmar Sound! I wonder where you'll find a richer grain region. There are fields upon fields, just like here in Skåne. The soil is so good that I cannot imagine anything that couldn't grow there."

"I can't help that," little Mats insisted. "I'm only relating what others have said before."

"And I have heard many say that there is not a more beautiful coast land than Tjust. Think of the bays and islets; of the manors and the groves!" said Osa. "Yes, that's true enough," little Mats admitted. "And don't you remember," continued Osa, "the school teacher said that such a lively and picturesque district as that bit of Småland which lies south of Lake Vettern is not to be found in all Sweden? Think of the beautiful lake and the yellow coast-mountains, and of Grenna and Jönköping, with its match factory, and think of Huskvarna, and all the big establishments there!" "Yes, that's true enough," said little Mats once again. "And think of Visingsö, little Mats, with the ruins and the oak forests and the legends! Think of the valley through which Em River flows, with all the villages and flour-mills and sawmills and carpenter shops!" "Yes, that is true enough," said little Mats, and seemed troubled.

All of a sudden he looked up and said: "Now we are pretty stupid! All this, of course, lies in Our Lord's Småland, in that part of the land which was already finished when Saint Peter undertook the job. It's only natural that it should be pretty and fine there. But in Saint Peter's Småland it looks as it says in the legend. And it wasn't surprising that Our Lord was distressed when he saw it," continued little Mats, picking up the thread of his story. "Saint Peter didn't lose his courage, at all events, but tried to comfort Our Lord. 'Don't be so grieved over this!' he said. 'Only wait until I have created people who can till the swamps and break up fields from the stone hills.'

"That was the end of Our Lord's patience — and he said: 'No! you can go down to Skåne and make the Skåninge, but the Smålander I shall create myself.' And so Our Lord created the Smålander, and made him quick-witted and contented and happy and thrifty and enterprising and capable, that he might be able to get his living in his poor country."

Then little Mats was silent; and if Nils Holgersson had also kept still, all would have gone well; but he couldn't possibly refrain from asking how Saint Peter had succeeded in creating the Skåninge.

"Well, what do you think yourself?" said little Mats, and he looked so scornful that Nils fell upon him, to thrash him. But Mats was only a little chap, and Osa, the goose-girl, who was a year older than he, ran forward instantly to help him. Good-natured though she was, she sprang like a lion as soon as any one touched her brother.

Nils Holgersson did not care to fight a girl, so turned his back; and he didn't look at those Småland children for the rest of the day.

Chapter Sixteen

THE CROWS

THE EARTHEN CROCK

IN THE southwest corner of Småland lies a parish called Sonnerbo — a rather smooth and even country. And one who sees it in winter, when it is covered with snow, cannot imagine that there is anything under the snow but garden-plots, rye-fields, and clover-meadows, as is generally the case in flat countries. But, in the beginning of April, when the snow melts away in Sonnerbo, it becomes apparent that under it lie only dry, sandy heaths, bare rocks, and big, marshy swamps. There are fields here and there, to be sure, but these are so small that they are scarcely worth mentioning; and there are also little red or gray farmhouses hidden away in some birch-coppice — almost as if they were afraid to be seen.

Where Sonnerbo Parish touches the boundaries of Halland, there is a sandy heath which is so far-reaching that he who stands at one end of it cannot look across to the other. Nothing except heather grows on the heath, and it wouldn't be easy to coax other growths to thrive there. To start with, one would have to uproot the heather; for it is thus with heather: although it has only a little shrunken root, small shrunken branches, and dry, shrunken leaves, it fancies itself a tree. Therefore, it acts just like real trees — spreads itself out in forest fashion over wide areas; holds faithfully together, and causes all foreign growths that wish to crowd in upon its territory to die out.

The only place on the heath where the heather is not all-powerful is a low, stony ridge which crosses it. There you'll find juniper bushes, mountain ash, and a few large, fine oaks. At the time that Nils travelled around with the wild geese, a little cabin stood there, with a bit of cleared ground around it. But the people who once lived there for some reason or other had moved away. The little cabin was empty now, and the ground lay unused.

On leaving the cabin the tenants had closed the damper, fastened the window-hooks, and locked the door. But no one had thought of the broken window-pane which was only stopped up with a rag. After the showers of a couple of summers, the rag had moulded and shrunk, and, finally, a crow had succeeded in poking it out.

The ridge on the heather-heath was really not so desolate as one might think, for it was inhabited by a large crow-folk. Naturally, the crows did not live there all the year around. They moved to foreign lands in the winter; in the autumn they travelled from one grain-field to another over all Gotaland, and picked grain; during the summer, they spread themselves over the farms in Sonnerbo Parish, and lived upon eggs and berries and birdlings; but every spring, at nesting time, they came back to the heather-heath.

The one who had poked the rag from the window was a crow-cock named Garm Whitefeather; but he was never called anything but Fumle or Drumle, or out and out Fumle-Drumle, because he always acted awkwardly and stupidly, and wasn't good for anything except to be made fun of. Fumle-Drumle was bigger and stronger than any of the other crows, but that didn't help him in the least; he was —

and remained — a butt for ridicule. Nor did it profit him that he came of very good stock. By rights he should have been leader for the whole flock, since this honour from time immemorial had belonged to the oldest Whitefeather. But long before Fumle-Drumle was born, the power had gone from his family, and it was now held by a cruel wild crow named Wind-Rush.

This transference of power was due to the fact that the crows on crow-ridge had decided to change their manner of living. Possibly there are many who think that everything in the shape of crow lives in the same way; but such is not the case. There are entire crow-folk who lead respectable lives — that is to say, they eat only grain, worms, caterpillars, and dead animals; and there are others who lead a regular bandit's life, who throw themselves upon baby hares and small birds, and who plunder every bird's nest they set eyes on.

The ancient Whitefeathers had been strict and temperate; and so long as they had led the flock, the crows had been compelled to conduct themselves in such a way that other birds could speak no ill of them. But the crows were numerous, and poverty was great among them. They didn't care to go the whole length of living a strictly moral life, so they rebelled against the Whitefeathers, and gave the power to Wind-Rush who was the worst nest-plunderer and robber that could be imagined — if his wife, Wind-Air, wasn't worse still. Under their government the crows had begun to lead such a life that now they were more feared than pigeon-hawks and leech-owls.

Naturally, Fumle-Drumle had nothing to say in the flock. The crows were all of the opinion that he did not in the least take after his forefathers, and that he wouldn't do as a leader. No one would have noticed him, if he hadn't constantly committed fresh blunders. A few, who were quite sensible, said that perhaps it was lucky for Fumle-Drumle that he was such a bungling idiot; otherwise Wind-Rush and Wind-Air would hardly have allowed him, who was of the old chieftain stock, to remain with the flock.

Now, on the other hand, they were rather friendly toward him, and willingly took him along with them on their marauding explorations, where all could observe how much more skilful and daring they were than he.

None of the crows knew that it was Fumle-Drumle who had pecked the rag out of the window; for had they known of this, they would have been very much astonished. Such a thing as daring to approach a human habitation they had never credited him with. He had kept this very carefully to himself, and he had his own good reasons for doing so. Wind and Air always treated him well in the daytime, and when the others were around. But one dark night, when the comrades were perched on the night branch, he was attacked by a couple of crows and nearly murdered. After that every night, when it was dark, he moved from his usual sleeping quarters into the empty cabin.

Now one afternoon, when the crows on the crow-ridge had put their nests in order, they happened upon a remarkable find. Wind-Rush, Fumle-Drumle, and a couple of the others had flown down into a big hollow in one corner of the heath. The hollow was nothing but a gravel-pit, but the crows could not be satisfied with such a simple explanation; they flew down into it continually, turning over every single sand-grain to get at the reason why human beings had dug it. While the crows were pottering around down there, a mass of gravel fell from one side. They rushed up to it, and had the good fortune to find amongst the fallen stones and stubble a large earthen crock, which was locked with a wooden clasp. Naturally, they wanted to know if there was anything in it, and tried to peck holes in the crock and to bend up the clasp, but had no success.

They stood perplexed looking at the crock, when they heard some one say: "Shall I come down and assist you crows?" They glanced up quickly. On the edge of the hollow sat a fox blinking down at them. He was one of the prettiest foxes as to both colour and form that they had ever seen. The only fault with him was that he had lost an ear.

"If you wish to do us a service, we will not say nay," said Wind-Rush, as he and the others flew up from the hollow. Then the fox jumped down in their place, pecked at the jar and pulled at the lock — but he couldn't open it either.

"Can you make out what there is in it?" said Wind-Rush. The fox rolled the jar back and forth, and listened carefully. "It must be silver money," said he.

This was more than the crows had expected. "Do you think it can be silver?" they gasped, their eyes ready to pop out of their heads with greed; for remarkable as it may sound, there is nothing in the world which crows love so much as silver.

"Hear how it rattles!" said the fox, rolling the crock around once more. "Only I can't understand how we shall get at it." "That will surely be impossible," said the crows. The fox stood rubbing his head against his left fore-leg, and pondered: Now perhaps he might succeed, with the help of the crows, in mastering that little imp who was always eluding him. "Oh! I know some one who can open the crock for you," said the fox. "Then tell us! Tell us!" cried the crows; and they were so excited that they tumbled down into the pit. "That I will do, if you'll first promise me that you will agree to my terms," he said.

Then the fox told the crows about Thumbietot, and said that if they could only bring him to the heath he would open the crock for them. But in payment for this counsel, he demanded that they should deliver Thumbietot to him as soon as he had got the silver money for them. The crows had no reason to spare Thumbietot, so accepted the proposal at once. It was easy enough to agree to this; but it was not so easy to find out where Thumbietot and the wild geese were stopping.

Wind-Rush himself started away with fifty crows, and said that he should soon return. But one day after another passed without the crows on the crow-ridge seeing a shadow of him.

KIDNAPPED BY CROWS

Wednesday, April thirteenth.

THE wild geese were up at daybreak, in time to get themselves a bite of food before starting out on their journey toward Östergotland. The island in Goose Bay, where they had slept, was small and barren, but in the water all around it were water-weeds upon which they could eat their fill. It was worse for the boy, however. He couldn't manage to find anything eatable.

As he stood there, hungry and drowsy, looking around in all directions, his glance fell upon a pair of squirrels playing upon the wooded point, opposite the rock island. He wondered if the squirrels had any of their winter supplies left, and asked the white goosey-gander to take him over to the point that he might beg them for a couple of hazelnuts.

The white one promptly swam across the bay with the boy, but as luck would have it, the squirrels were having so much fun chasing each other from tree to tree that they didn't bother about listening to him. Instead they drew farther into the grove. He hurried after them, and was soon out of the goosey-gander's sight — the latter stayed behind and waited on the shore.

The boy was wading forward between some white crocus-stems — which were so high that they reached to his chin — when he felt some one from behind catch hold of him, and try to lift him up. He faced about and saw that a crow had gripped him by the shirt-band. He tried to jerk himself loose, but before he could do so, another crow rushed up, caught him by the stocking, and knocked him over.

If Nils had at once cried for help, the white goosey-gander certainly could have saved him; but the boy probably thought that he could protect himself, unaided, against a couple of crows. He kicked and struck out, but the crows didn't let go their hold, and succeeded in rising into the air with him. To make matters worse, they flew so recklessly that his head struck a branch. He got such a hard bump that it grew black before his eyes, and he lost consciousness.

When he opened his eyes once more, he found himself high above the ground. He regained his senses slowly; at first he knew neither where he was, nor what he saw. When he glanced down, he noticed that under him was spread a tremendously big woolly carpet which was woven in greens and reds, and in large irregular patterns. The carpet was very thick and fine, but he thought it a pity that it had been so badly used. It was actually ragged; long tears ran through it and, in some places, large pieces were torn away. But strangest of all, it was spread over a mirror-floor; for under the holes and tears in the carpet shone bright and glittering glass.

And then, the boy saw the sun come rolling up in the heavens. Instantly, the mirror-glass under the holes and tears in the carpet began to shimmer in red and gold. It looked gorgeous, and the boy was charmed with the pretty colour-scheme, although he didn't exactly understand what it was that he saw. But now the crows descended and at once he understood that the big carpet under him was the earth, which was dressed in green cone-trees and brown, naked leaf-trees, and that the holes and tears were shimmering bays and little lakes.

He remembered that the first time he had travelled up in the air, he had thought that the earth in Skåne looked like a piece of checked cloth. But this landscape, which resembled a torn carpet — what country might this be?

He began to ask himself a lot of questions. Why wasn't he sitting on the goosey-gander's back? Why did a great swarm of crows fly around him? And why was he being pulled and knocked hither and thither so that he was about to break in two.

Then, all at once, the whole thing dawned upon him. He had been kidnapped by a couple of crows. The white goosey-gander was still on the shore, waiting, and to-day the wild geese were to travel to Ostergötland. He was being carried southwest; this he understood because the sun's disc was behind him. The big forest-carpet which lay beneath him was surely Småland.

"What will become of the goosey-gander now, when I cannot look after him?" thought the boy; and he began to shout at the crows to take him back to the wild geese instantly. He was not at all uneasy on his own account for he believed that they were carrying him off simply in a spirit of mischief.

The crows didn't pay the slightest attention to his exhortations, but flew on as fast as they could. After a bit, one of them flapped his wings in a manner which meant: "Look out! Danger!" Soon thereafter they came down in a spruce forest, pushed their way between prickly branches to the ground, and put the boy down under a thick pine, where he was so well concealed that not even a falcon could have sighted him.

Fifty crows, with bills pointed toward him, surrounded him. "Now, crows, perhaps I may hear what your purpose is in carrying me off," said he. But he was hardly allowed to finish the sentence before a big crow hissed at him: "Keep still! or I'll bore your eyes out!"

It was plain that the crow meant what she said; and there was nothing for the boy to do but obey. So he sat there and stared at the crows, and the crows stared at him.

The longer he looked at them, the less he liked them. Their feather-dresses were shockingly dusty and unkempt — as if they had never come in contact with water or oil. Their toes and claws were grimy with dried-in mud, and the corners of their mouths were covered with food drippings. These were very different birds from the wild geese — that he observed. He thought they had a cruel, sneaky, watchful, and bold appearance, just like cut-throats and vagabonds.

"I have certainly fallen in with a real robber-band," he remarked to himself.

Just then he heard the wild geese's call above him.

"Where are you? Here am I. Where are you? Here am I."

He understood that Akka and the others were out searching for him; but before he could answer them, the big crow, who appeared to be the leader of the band, hissed in his ear: "Think of your eyes!" And there was nothing for him to do but to keep still.

He heard their call once or twice more, then it died away. The wild geese did not know he was so near them. "Well, you'll have to get along by yourself, Nils Holgersson," he thought. "Now you must prove whether or not you have learned anything during these weeks in the open."

A moment later the crows gave the signal to break up; and since it was still their intention, apparently, to carry him along in such a way that one held onto his shirt-band, and one to a stocking, the boy said: "Is there not one among you strong enough to carry me on his back? You have already travelled so badly with me that I feel as if I were in pieces. Only let me ride! I'll not jump from the crow's back, that I promise you."

"Oh! you needn't think that we mind how you fare," snapped the leader. But now the largest of the crows, a dishevelled and uncouth one with a white feather in his wing, came forward and said: "It would certainly be best for all of us, Wind-Rush, if Thumbietot got there whole, rather than in sections. Therefore, I shall carry him on my back." "If you can do it, Fumle-Drumle, I have no objection," said Wind-Rush. "But don't lose him!"

Herewith much was already gained, and the boy actually felt contented. "There is nothing to be gained by losing my grit because I have been kidnapped by the crows,"

"... IS THERE NOT ONE AMONG YOU STRONG ENOUGH TO CARRY ME ON HIS BACK?"

thought he. "I'll surely be able to manage those poor little wretches."

The crows continued to fly southwest, over Småland. It was a glorious morning — sunny and calm, and the birds down on the earth were singing their best love songs. In a high, dark forest sat the thrush himself, with drooping wings and swelling throat; and he struck up a tune. "How pretty you are! How pretty you are! How pretty you are!" sang he. "No one is so pretty. No one is so pretty. No one is so pretty." As soon as he had finished this song, he began all over again.

But just then the boy rode over the forest; and when he had heard the song a couple of times, and marked that the thrush knew no other, he put both hands up to his mouth as a speaking trumpet, and called down: "We've heard all this before. We've heard all this before." "Who is it? Who is it? Who is it? Who makes fun of me?" asked the thrush trying to catch a glimpse of the one who called. "It is Kidnapped-by-Crows who makes fun of your song," answered the boy. At that, the crow-chief turned his head and said: "Be careful of your eyes, Thumbietot!" But the boy thought, "Oh! I don't care about that. I want to show you that I'm not afraid of you!"

They travelled farther and farther inland with woods and lakes everywhere. In a birch-grove on a naked bough sat Mrs. Wood-Dove; before her stood Mr. Wood-Dove. He blew up his feathers, cocked his head, raised and lowered his body, until the breast-feathers rattled against the branch. And all the while he cooed: "You, you, you are the loveliest in all the forest. No one in the forest is so lovely as you, you, you!"

But up in the air the boy rode past, and when he heard

Mr. Dove he couldn't keep still. "Don't you believe him! Don't you believe him!" cried he.

"Who, who, who, is it that lies about me?" cooed Mr. Dove, and tried to get a sight of the one who shrieked at him. "It is Caught-by-Crows that lies about you," replied the boy. Again Wind-Rush turned to the boy and commanded him to shut up, but Fumle-Drumle, who was carrying him, said: "Let him chatter, then all the little birds will think that we crows have become quick-witted and funny birds." "Oh! they're not such fools as that," said Wind-Rush; but he liked the idea just the same, for after that he let the boy call out as much as he liked.

They flew mostly over forests and woodlands. In one place they saw a pretty old manor-house with the lake before it, and the forest behind it. The old house had red walls and a turreted roof; great sycamores about the grounds, and big, thick gooseberry-bushes in the orchard. On top of the weathercock sat the starling, singing so loud that every note was heard by the wife, who sat on an egg in the heart of a pear tree. "We have four pretty little eggs," sang the starling. "We have four pretty little round eggs. We have the whole nest filled with fine eggs."

When the starling sang the song for the thousandth time, the boy rode over the place. He put his hands up to his mouth, as a pipe, and called to the starling: "The magpie will get them. The magpie will get them."

"Who is it that wants to frighten me?" asked the starling, and flapped his wings uneasily. "It is Captured-by-Crows that frightens you," said the boy. This time the crow-chief didn't attempt to hush him up. Indeed both he and his flock were having so much fun that they cawed with satisfaction.

The farther inland they came, the larger were the lakes, and the more plentiful the islands and points. And on a lake-shore stood a drake bowing before the duck. "I'll be true to you all the days of my life. I'll be true to you all the days of my life," vowed the drake. "It won't last until the summer's end," shrieked the boy. "Who are you?" called the drake. "My name's Stolen-by-Crows," shrieked the boy.

At dinner time the crows lighted in a food-grove. They walked about and procured food for themselves, but none of them thought of giving the boy anything. Then Fumle-Drumle came riding up to the chief with a dog-rose branch with a few dried buds on it. "Here's something for you, Wind-Rush," said he. "This is dainty food, and suitable for you." Wind-Rush sniffed contemptuously. "Do you think that I want to eat old, dry buds?" said he. "And I thought you would be pleased with them!" said Fumle-Drumle, throwing away the dog-rose branch as if in despair. It fell right in front of the boy, and he wasn't slow in grabbing it and eating until he was satisfied.

When the crows were done eating, they began to chatter. "What are you thinking about, Wind-Rush? You are so quiet to-day," said one of them to the leader. "I'm thinking that once upon a time there lived in this district a hen who was very fond of her mistress; and in order to really please her, she went and laid a nest full of eggs, which she hid under the storehouse floor. The mistress of the house wondered, of course, where the hen was keeping herself such a long time. She searched for her, but did not find her. Can you guess, Longbill, who it was that found her and the eggs?"

"I think I can guess it, Wind-Rush, but when you have

told about this, I will tell you something like it. Do you remember the big, black cat in Hinneryd's parish house? She was dissatisfied because they always took the newborn kittens from her, and drowned them. Just once did she succeed in keeping them concealed, and that was when she had lain them in a haystack out of doors. She was pretty well pleased with those young kittens, but I believe that I got more pleasure out of them than she did."

Now they became so excited that they all talked at once. "What kind of a trick is that — to steal little kittens?" said one. "I once chased a young hare who was almost full-grown. That meant to follow him from covert to covert." He got no further before another took the words from him. "It may be sport, perhaps, to annoy hens and cats, but I find it still more remarkable that a crow can worry a human being. I once stole a silver spoon ——"

But now the boy thought he was too good to sit and hear such gabble. "Now listen to me, you crows!" said he. "I say that you ought to be ashamed of bragging about all your wickedness. I have lived amongst wild geese for three weeks, and while with them I never heard or saw anything but good. You must have a bad chief, since he permits you to rob and murder in this way. You should really begin life anew, for I can tell you that human beings have grown so tired of your wickedness that they are doing everything in their power to root you out. And there will soon be an end to you."

When Wind-Rush and the crows heard this, they were so furious that they wanted to throw themselves upon him and tear him in pieces. But Fumle-Drumle laughed and cawed, and stood in front of him. "Oh, no, no!" said he, and seemed perfectly horrified. "What think you that

Wind-Air will say if you tear Thumbietot in pieces before he has got that silver money for us?" "It has to be you, Fumle-Drumle, that's afraid of women-folk," said Rush. But, at any rate, both he and the others left Thumbietot in peace.

Shortly after that the crows moved on. Until now the boy had thought that Småland wasn't such a poor country after all. Of course it was woody and full of mountain-ridges, but alongside the islands and lakes lay cultivated grounds, and any real desolation he hadn't come upon. But the farther inland they went the fewer became the villages and cottages. Toward the last, he thought he was riding over a veritable wilderness of nothing but swamps and heaths and juniper-hills.

The sun had gone down, but it was still quite light when the crows reached the large heather-heath. Wind-Rush sent a crow ahead to say that he had met with success; and when it was known, Wind-Air, with several hundred crows from crow-ridge, flew to meet the arrivals. In the midst of the deafening cawing which the crows emitted, Fumle-Drumle said to the boy: "You have been so comical and so jolly during the trip that I am really fond of you. Therefore, I want to give you some good advice. As soon as we light, you'll be requested to do a bit of work which may seem very easy to you; but beware of doing it!"

Soon thereafter Fumle-Drumle put Nils down in the bottom of a sand-pit. The boy flung himself on his back, and lay there as though he were simply done up. Such a lot of crows fluttered about him that the air rustled like a windstorm, but he didn't look up.

"Thumbietot," said Wind-Rush, "get up now! You shall help us with a matter which will be very easy for you."

The boy didn't move, but pretended to be asleep. Then Wind-Rush took him by the arm and dragged him over the sand toward an earthen crock of old-time make that stood in the pit. "Get up, Thumbietot," said he, "and open this crock!" "Why can't you let me sleep!" yawned the boy. "I'm too tired to do anything to-night. Wait until to-morrow!"

"Open the crock!" said Wind-Rush, shaking him. "How shall a poor little child be able to open such a crock? Why, it's quite as large as I am myself." "Open it!" commanded Wind-Rush once more, "or it will be a sorry thing for you." The boy got up, tottered over to the crock, fumbled the clasp, and let his arms fall. "I'm not usually so weak," he said. "If you will only let me sleep until morning, I think that I'll be able to manage with that clasp."

But Wind-Rush was impatient, and he flew at the boy and nipped him in the leg. The boy didn't care to suffer that sort of treatment from a crow. He jerked himself loose, ran a couple of paces backward, drew his knife from the sheath, and held it threateningly in front of him. "You'd better be careful!" he cried to Wind-Rush.

But Wind-Rush, too, was so enraged that he didn't dodge the danger. He rushed at the boy, just as if he were blind, and ran so straight against the knife that it entered through his eye into his head. The boy quickly drew the knife back, but Wind-Rush only struck out with his wings, then fell dead.

"Wind-Rush is dead! The stranger has killed our chieftain, Wind-Rush!" cried the nearest crows. And then there was a terrible uproar. Some wailed, others cried for vengeance. They all ran or fluttered up to the boy, with Fumle-Drumle in the lead. But Fumle-Drumle acted badly, as usual, fluttering and spreading his wings over the boy, and preventing the others from coming forward and running their bills into him.

The boy thought that now things looked bad for him. He couldn't run away from the crows, and there was no place where he could hide. Suddenly he happened to think of the earthen crock. He took a firm hold on the clasp and pulled it out. Then he hopped into the crock to hide there. But the crock was a poor hiding-place, for it was filled almost to the brim with little, thin silver coins. The boy couldn't get far enough down, so he stooped and began to throw out the coins.

Until now the crows had fluttered around him in a thick swarm, pecking at him, but when he threw out the money they immediately forgot their thirst for vengeance, and hurried to gather the coins. The boy threw out handfuls and all the crows — yes, even Wind-Air herself — picked them up. And each one as he succeeded in picking up a coin ran off to the nest with the utmost speed to conceal it.

After the boy had thrown out all the silver pennies from the crock he glanced up. But one crow was left in the sand-pit. That was Fumle-Drumle, with the white feather in his wing; he who had carried Thumbietot. "You have rendered me a greater service than you yourself understand," said the crow in a tone very different from the one he had used hitherto, "and I want to save your life. Sit down on my back, and I'll take you to a hiding-place where you will be safe to-night. To-morrow, I shall arrange it so that you can get back to the wild geese."

THE CABIN

Thursday, April fourteenth.

THE following morning when the boy awoke, he was lying in a bed. When he saw that he was in a house, with four walls around him, and a roof over him, he thought that he was at home. "I wonder if mother will come soon with some coffee," he muttered to himself where he lay, half awake. Then he remembered that he was in a deserted cabin on the crow-ridge and that Fumle-Drumle with the white feather had borne him there the night before.

The boy was sore all over after the journey he had made, and he thought it lovely to lie still while waiting for Fumle-Drumle, who had promised to come and fetch him.

Curtains of checked cotton hung before the bed. He drew them aside to look out into the cabin and instantly it occurred to him that he had never seen the mate to a cabin like this. The walls consisted of nothing but two rows of logs; then the roof began. There was no interior ceiling, so he could look clear up to the roof-tree. The cabin was so small that it appeared to be built for such as he rather than for real people. However, the fireplace and chimney were so large, he thought he had never seen larger. The entrance door was in a gable-wall at the side of the fireplace, and so narrow that it was more like a wicket than a door. In the other gable-wall he saw a low and broad window with many little panes. There was scarcely any movable furniture in the cabin. The bench by the wall and the table under the window were stationary — also the big bed where he lay, and the many-coloured cupboard.

The boy could not help wondering who owned the cabin, and why it was deserted. It certainly looked as though the people who had lived there expected to return. The coffee-urn and the gruel-pot stood on the hearth, and there was wood in the fireplace; in a corner stood the oven rake and baker's peel; the spinning-wheel was raised on a bench; on the shelf over the window lay oakum and flax, two skeins of yarn, a candle, and a bunch of matches.

Yes, it surely looked as if the people who had lived there intended to come back. There were bedclothes on the bed; and the walls were hung with long strips of cloth, upon which three riders named Kaspar, Melchior, and Balthazar were painted. The same horses and riders were pictured many times. They rode all around the cabin, and even up toward the joists.

But in the roof the boy saw something which brought him to his feet in a jiffy. Two big bread-cakes hung there upon a spit. They looked old and mouldy, but it was bread all the same. He gave them a knock with the oven-rake and one cake fell to the floor. He ate some of it, then filled his bag. It was incredible how good bread was, anyhow.

He looked around the cabin once more, trying to discover if there was anything else he might find useful to take along. "I may as well take what I need, since no one else cares about it," thought he. But most everything was too big and heavy. All that he could carry might be a few matches, perhaps.

He clambered upon the table, and swung himself, with the help of the curtains, onto the window-shelf. While he stood there stuffing the matches into his bag, the crow with the white feather came in through the window. "Well, here I am at last," said Fumle-Drumle as he lit on the table. "I couldn't get here any sooner because we crows have elected a new chieftain in Wind-Rush's place." "Whom have you chosen?" asked the boy. "Well, we have chosen one who will not permit robbery and injustice. We have elected Garm Whitefeather, lately called Fumle-Drumle," he answered, drawing himself up until he looked absolutely regal. "That was a good choice," said the boy, and congratulated him. "You may well wish me luck!" said Garm; then he told the boy about the time they had had with Wind-Rush and Wind-Air.

During this recital the boy heard a voice outside the window which he thought sounded familiar. "Is he here?" inquired the fox. "Yes, he's hidden in there," answered a crow-voice. "Be careful, Thumbietot!" cried Garm. "Wind-Air stands outside with that fox who wants to eat you." More he didn't have time to say, for just then Smirre dashed against the window. The old, rotten window-frame gave way. The next second Smirre stood on the window-table and Garm Whitefeather, who had no time to fly away, he instantly killed. Thereupon he jumped to the floor, and looked around for the boy. Thumbietot tried to hide behind a big oakum-spiral, but Smirre had already spied him, and was crouched for the final spring. Since the cabin was so small and so low, the boy realized that the fox would have no difficulty in reaching him. But at that moment the boy was not without weapons of defence. He quickly struck a match, set it to the oakum, and when it was aflame he threw it down upon Smirre Fox. As the fire enveloped the fox, he was seized with mad terror. He thought no more about the boy, but rushed wildly out of the cabin.

But it looked as if the boy had escaped one danger only to throw himself into a greater one. From the tuft of oakum which he had flung at Smirre the fire had spread to the bedhangings. He jumped down and tried to smother it, but now it blazed too violently. The cabin was soon filled with smoke, and Smirre Fox, who had remained just outside the window, began to grasp the state of affairs within. "Well, Thumbietot," he called out, "which do you choose now: to be broiled alive in there, or to come out here to me? Of course, I should prefer to have the pleasure of eating you; but in whichever way death meets you it will be dear to me."

The boy could not think but that the fox was right, for the fire was making rapid headway. The whole bed was now ablaze; smoke rose from the floor; and along the painted wall-strips the fire crept from rider to rider. The boy had jumped up into the fireplace and was trying to open the oven door, when some one inserted a key into the keyhole and slowly turned the lock. "It must be human beings coming," he thought. And in his dire dilemma he was not afraid, but only glad. He was already on the threshold when the door opened. Before him stood two children. How they looked when they saw the cabin in flames he took no time to find out, but rushed past them into the open.

He didn't dare run far. He knew, of course, that Smirre Fox lay in wait for him, and he understood that he must remain near the children. He turned to see what sort of folk they were, but he hadn't looked at them a second before he ran up to them and cried: "Oh, good-day, Osa goose-girl! Oh, good-day, little Mats!"

For when the boy saw those children he forgot entirely where he was. Crows and burning cabin and talking animals had vanished from his memory. He was walking on a stubble-field in West Vemmenhög tending a goose-flock; and beside him, on the field, walked those same Småland children, with their geese. The instant he recognized them he bounded to the stone-hedge and shouted: "Oh, good-day, Osa goose-girl! Oh, good-day, little Mats!"

But when the children saw such a little creature coming up to them with outstretched hands, they caught hold of each other, staggered back, and looked scared to death.

When the boy observed their terror he came to and remembered who he was. And then it seemed to him that nothing worse could happen than that those children should see how he had been bewitched. Shame and grief because he was no longer a human being overpowered him. He turned and fled — he knew not whither.

But a glad meeting awaited the boy when he came down to the heath. For there, in the heather, he spied something white, and toward him came the white goosey-gander, accompanied by Dunfin. When the white one saw the boy running with such speed, he thought that dreadful fiends were pursuing him. So he hastily flung him upon his back and flew off with him.

CHAPTER SEVENTEEN

THE OLD PEASANT WOMAN

Thursday, April fourteenth.

THREE tired wanderers were out in the late evening in search of a night harbour. They travelled over a poor and desolate portion of northern Småland. But the sort of resting-place they wanted, they should have been able to find; for they were no weaklings who asked for soft beds or comfortable rooms. "If one of these long mountain-ridges had a peak so high and steep that a fox couldn't in any way climb up to it, then we should have a good sleeping-place," said one. "If a single one of the big swamps was thawed out, and so marshy and wet that a fox wouldn't dare venture out on it, that, too, would be a right good night harbour," said the second. "If the ice on one of the large lakes over which we travel were only loose, so that a fox could not come out upon it, then we should have found just what we are seeking," said the third.

The worst of it was that when the sun went down two of the travellers became so sleepy that every second they were ready to fall to the ground. The third, who could keep awake, grew more and more uneasy as night approached. "Then it was a misfortune that we came to a land where lakes and swamps are frozen, so that a fox can get around everywhere. In other places the ice has melted away; but now we're well up in the very coldest Småland, where spring has not as yet arrived. I don't know how I shall ever manage to find a good sleeping-place! Unless I find some spot that is well protected, Smirre Fox will be upon us before morning."

He gazed in all directions, but saw no shelter where he could lodge. It was a dark and chilly night, with wind and drizzle. It grew more terrible and disagreeable around him every second.

This may sound strange, perhaps, but the travellers did not seem to have the least desire to ask for house-room on any farm. They had already passed many parishes without knocking at a single door. Little hillside cabins on the outskirts of the forest, which all poor wanderers are glad to run across, they took no notice of either. One might almost be tempted to say they deserved to have a hard time of it, since they did not seek help where it was to be had for the asking.

But finally, when it was so dark that there was scarcely a glimmer of light left under the skies and the two who needed rest journeyed on in a kind of half-sleep, they happened upon a farmyard which was far removed from all neighbouring farms. Not only did it lie there desolate, but it appeared to be uninhabited as well. No smoke rose from the chimney; no light shone through the windows; no human being moved on the place. When the one who could keep awake saw the place, he thought: "Now come what may, we must try to get in here. Anything better we are not likely to find."

Soon after that, all three stood in the houseyard. Two of them fell asleep the instant they stood still, but the third looked about him eagerly, to find out where they could get under cover. It was not a small farm. Beside the dwelling house and stable and smokehouse, there were long ranges with granaries and storehouses and cattlesheds. But it all looked awfully poor and dilapidated. The houses had gray, moss-grown, leaning walls, which seemed ready to topple over. In the roofs were yawning holes, and the doors hung aslant on broken hinges. It was apparent that here no one had taken the trouble to drive a nail into a wall in a long time.

Meanwhile, he who was awake had discovered which of the houses was the cowshed. He roused his travelling companions from their sleep, and conducted them to the cowshed door. Luckily, this was not fastened with anything but a hasp which he could easily push up with a rod. He heaved a sigh of relief at the thought that they should soon be in safety. But as the cowshed door swung open with a sharp creaking sound, he heard a cow begin to bellow. "Are you coming at last, mistress?" said she. "I thought you were not going to give me any supper to-night."

The one who was awake paused in the doorway, terror-stricken, when he discovered that the cowshed was not empty. But he soon saw that there was only one cow in the shed, and three or four chickens; and then he took courage again. "We are three poor travellers who want to come in somewhere, where no fox can assail us, and no human being capture us," said he. "We wonder if this can be a good place for us." "I cannot believe but that it is," answered the cow. "To be sure the walls are wretched, but the fox does not walk through them as yet; and no one lives here but an old peasant woman, who isn't at all likely to make a captive of any one. But who are you?" she continued, as she twisted in her stall to get a sight of the newcomers. "I am Nils Holgersson from Vemmenhog, who has been transformed into an elf," replied the first of the incomers, "and I have with me a tame goose, whom I usually ride, and a gray goose." "Such distinguished guests have never before been within my four walls," said the cow, "and I bid you welcome, although I would have preferred that it had been my mistress, come to give me my supper."

The boy led the geese into the cowshed, which was rather large, and placed them in an empty manger, where they fell asleep instantly. For himself, he made a little bed of straw thinking that he, too, would drop to sleep at once.

But this was impossible, for the poor cow, who hadn't had her supper, wasn't still an instant. She shook her flanks, moved around in the stall, complaining all the while of how hungry she was. The boy couldn't get a wink of sleep, but lay there thinking over all that had happened to him during these last days.

He thought of Osa, the goose-girl, and little Mats, whom he had so unexpectedly encountered; and it occurred to him that the little cabin which he had set on fire must have been their old home in Småland. Now he remembered that he had heard them speak of just such a cabin, and of the big heather-heath which lay below it. They had wandered back there to see their old home again, and when they arrived, it was in flames.

It was indeed a great sorrow that he had brought upon them, and it hurt him very much. If he ever again became a human being, he would try to make up for all this damage and miscalculation.

Then his thoughts wandered to the crows. And when he thought of Fumle-Drumle who had saved his life, and who had met his own death so soon after having been elected chieftain, he was so distressed that tears filled his eyes.

He had had a pretty rough time of it these last few days.

But anyhow it was a rare stroke of luck that the goosey-gander and Dunfin had found him.

The goosey-gander had said that as soon as the wild geese discovered that Thumbietot had disappeared, they had asked all the small animals in the forest about him. They soon learned that a flock of Småland crows had carried him off. But the crows were already out of sight, and whither they had directed their course no one had been able to say. That they might find the boy as soon as possible, Akka had commanded the wild geese to start out — two by two — in different directions, to search for him. But after a two days' hunt, whether or not they had found him, they were to meet in northwestern Småland on a high mountain-top, which resembled an abrupt, chopped-off tower, and was called Taberg. After Akka had given them the best directions, as to how they should reach Taberg, they had separated.

The white goosey-gander had chosen Dunfin as travelling companion, and they had flown hither and thither with the greatest anxiety for Thumbietot. During this ramble they had heard a thrush, who sat in a treetop, cry and wail that some one who called himself *Kidnapped-by-Crows* had made fun of him. They had talked with the thrush, and he had shown them in which direction that *Kidnapped-by-Crows* had travelled. Afterward, they had met a dove-cock, a starling, and a drake who had all wailed about a little culprit that had disturbed their song, and who was named *Caught-by-Crows*, *Captured-by-Crows*, and *Stolen-by-Crows*. In this way, they were enabled to trace Thumbietot all the way to the heather-heath in Sonnerbo Parish.

As soon as the goosey-gander and Dunfin had found

Thumbietot, they had flown northward, in order to reach Taberg. But it had been a long road to travel, and the darkness was upon them before they had sighted the mountain-top. "If we only get there by to-morrow, surely all our troubles will be over," thought the boy, as he dug down into the straw to have it warmer. All the while the cow fussed and fumed in the stall. Then, all of a sudden, she began to talk to the boy. "Everything is wrong with me," said the cow. "I am neither milked nor tended. I have no night fodder in my manger, and no bed has been made under me. My mistress came here at dusk, to put things in order for me, but she felt so ill that she had to go back to the cabin; and she has not returned."

"It's distressing that I should be little and powerless," said the boy. "I don't believe that I am able to help you." "You can't make me believe that you are powerless because you are little," said the cow. "All the elves that I've ever heard of were so strong that they could pull a whole load of hay, and strike a cow dead with one fist." The boy couldn't help laughing at the cow. "They were a very different kind of elf from me," he said. "But I'll loosen your halter and open the door for you, so that you can go out and drink in one of the pools on the place, and then I'll try to climb up to the hayloft and throw some hay down to you." "Yes, that would be some help," said the cow.

The boy did as he had said; and when the cow stood with a full manger in front of her, he thought that at last he should get some sleep. But he had hardly crept down into the bed before she began anew to talk to him.

"You'll be clean put out with me if I ask one thing more of you," said the cow. "Oh, no I won't, if it's only some-

"'YES, THAT WOULD BE SOME HELP,' SAID THE COW"

thing that I'm able to do," assured the boy. "Then I shall ask you to go into the cabin, directly opposite, to find out how my mistress is getting along. I fear some misfortune has come to her." "No! I can't do that," said the boy. "I dare not show myself before human beings." "Surely you're not afraid of an old and sick woman," said the cow. "But you do not have to go into the cabin. Just stand outside the door and peep through the crack!" "Oh! if that is all you ask of me, I'll do it, of course," said the boy.

With that he opened the cowshed door and went out into the yard. It was a fearful night! Neither moon nor stars shone; the wind blew a gale, and the rain came down in torrents. And worst of all was that seven great owls sat in a row under the eaves of the cabin. It was awful just to hear them, where they sat and grumbled at the weather; but it was even worse to think what would happen to him if one of them should set eyes on him. That would be the last of him.

"Pity him who is little!" said the boy as he ventured out. And he had a right to say this, for he was blown down twice before he got to the house: once the wind swept him into a pool which was so deep that he came near drowning. But he got there nevertheless.

He clambered up the steps, scrambled over the threshold, and came into the hallway. The cabin door was closed, but down in one corner a large piece had been cut away, to let the cat in and out. It was no difficulty whatever for the boy to see how things were in the cabin.

He had barely glanced in when he staggered back and turned his head away. An old gray-haired woman lay stretched on the floor within. She neither moved nor moaned; and her face shone strangely white. It was as if an invisible moon had cast a feeble light over it.

The boy remembered that when his grandfather had died, his face had also become so strangely white-like. And he understood that the old woman who lay on the cabin floor must be dead. Death had probably come to her so suddenly that she didn't even have time to lie down on her bed.

As he thought of being alone with the dead in the middle of the dark night, he was terribly afraid. He threw himself headlong down the steps, and rushed back to the cowshed.

When he told the cow of what he had seen in the cabin, she stopped eating. "So my mistress is dead," sighed she. "Then it will soon be over for me as well." "There will always be some one to look out for you," said the boy comfortingly. "Ah! you don't know," said the cow, "that I am already twice as old as a cow usually is before she is laid upon the slaughter-bench. But then, I do not wish to live any longer, since she, in there, can come no more to care for me."

She said nothing more for a time, but the boy observed that she neither slept nor ate. It was not long before she began to speak again. "Is she lying on the bare floor?" she asked. "She is," said the boy. "She had a habit of coming out to the cowshed," she continued, "and talking about everything that troubled her. I understood what she said, although I could not answer her. The last days she talked of how afraid she was that there would be no one with her when she died. She was troubled lest none be near to close her eyes and fold her hands across her breast, after she was dead. Perhaps you'll go in and do this?" The boy hesitated. He remembered that when his grandfather had died, mother had been very careful about putting everything to rights. He knew this was something which had to be done. But, on the other hand, he felt that he did not dare go to the dead, in the ghastly night. He didn't say no; nor did he take a step toward the cowshed door. For a couple of seconds the old cow was silent, as if waiting for an answer. But when the boy said nothing, she did not repeat her request. Instead, she began to talk to him of her mistress.

There was much to tell, first and foremost, about all the children she had brought up. They had been in the cowshed every day, and in the summer they had taken the cattle to pasture on the swamp and in the groves so the old cow knew all about them. They had been splendid, all of them, and happy and industrious. A cow knew well enough what her caretakers were good for.

There was also much to be said about the farm. It had not always been as poor as it was now, although the greater part of it consisted of swamps and stony groves. There was not much room left for fields, but there was plenty of good fodder everywhere. At one time there had been a cow for every stall in the cowshed; and the oxshed, which was now empty, had at one time been filled with oxen. And then there was life and gayety, both in cabin and cowhouse. When the mistress opened the cowshed door she always hummed or sang, and all the cows mooed their gladness when they heard her coming.

But the good man had died when the children were so small that they could be of no assistance, and the mistress had to take charge of the farm, and all the work and responsibility. She had been as strong as a man; and had both ploughed and reaped. Evenings, when she came into the cowshed to milk, sometimes she was so tired that she wept. But when she thought of her children she dashed away her tears, and was cheerful again. "It doesn't matter. Good times are coming again for me, too, if only my children grow up. Yes, if they only grow up."

But as soon as the children were grown, a strange longing came over them. They didn't want to stay at home, so they went away to a strange country. Their mother never got any help from them. A couple of her children were married before they went away, and they left their children behind, in the old home. And now these children accompanied the mistress to the cowshed, just as her own had done. They tended the cows, and were fine, good folk. And evenings, when the mistress was so tired out that she could have fallen asleep in the middle of the milking, she would arouse herself again to renewed courage by thinking of them. "Good times are coming for me, too," said she — and shook off sleep — "when once they are grown."

But when these children grew up, they went to their parents in the strange land. No one came back, no one stayed at home. The old mistress was left alone on the farm.

Probably she had never asked them to remain with her. "Think you, Redlinna, that I would ask them to stay here with me, when they can go out in the world and have things comfortable?" she would say as she stood in the stall with the old cow. "Here in Småland they have only poverty to look forward to."

But when the last grandchild was gone, it was all up with the mistress. All at once she became bent and gray, and tottered as she walked, as if she no longer had the strength to move about. She stopped working. She did not care to look after the farm, but let everything go to rack and ruin. She did not repair the houses; and she sold both cows and oxen. The only one she kept was the old cow who now talked with Thumbietot. Her she let live because all the children had tended her.

She could have taken maids and farm-hands into her service, who would have helped her with the work, but she couldn't bear to see strangers around her, since her own had deserted her. Perhaps she was better satisfied to let the farm go to ruin, since none of her children were coming back to take charge of it after she was gone. She did not mind being poor herself for she didn't value that which was only hers. But she was troubled lest the children should find out how hard she had it. "If only the children do not hear of this! If only the children do not hear of this!" she sighed as she tottered through the cowhouse.

The children wrote constantly, and begged her to come to them; but this she did not wish. She didn't want to see the land that had taken them from her. She was angry at it. "It's foolish of me, perhaps, that I do not like that land which has been so good for them," said she. "But, I don't want to see it."

She thought only of the children, and of this — that they must needs have gone. When summer came, she led the cow out to graze in the big swamp. All day she would sit at the edge of the swamp, her hands in her lap; and on the way home she would say: "You see, Redlinna, if there had been large, rich fields here, in place of these barren swamps, there would have been no need of their leaving."

She could become furious with the swamp which spread out so big, and did no good. She would sit and talk of how it was the swamp's fault that the children had left her.

The last evening she had been more trembly and feeble than ever. She could not even do the milking. She had leaned against the manger and talked about two strangers who had been to see her, and who had asked if they might buy the swamp. They wanted to drain it, they said, to raise grain on it. This had made her both anxious and happy. "Do you hear, Redlinna," she had said. "Do you hear that grain can grow on the swamp? Now I shall write to the children to come home. They won't have to stay away any longer; for now they can get their bread here at home." It was this that she had gone into the cabin to do ——

The boy heard no more. He had already opened the door, crossed the yard and gone in to the dead, of whom he had but lately been so afraid.

The cabin was not so bare as he had expected. It was well supplied with the sort of things one generally finds among those who have relatives in America. In a corner there was an American rocking chair; on the table before the window lay a brocaded plush cover; there was a pretty spread on the bed; on the walls, in carved-wood frames, hung the photographs of the children and grandchildren who had gone away; on the bureau stood high vases and a couple of candlesticks, with thick, spiral candles in them.

The boy searched for a matchbox and lighted these candles, not because he needed more light than he already had, but because he thought that this was one way to honour the dead.

Then he went up to the woman, closed her eyes, folded her hands across her breast, and stroked back the thin gray hair from her face.

He thought no more about being afraid of her, but he was deeply grieved because she had been forced to live out her old age in loneliness and longing. He, at least, would watch over her dead body this night.

He hunted up the psalm book, and sat down to read a couple of psalms in an undertone. But in the middle of the reading he paused, for he had begun to think of his mother and father.

Think, that parents can long so for their children! This he had never known. Think, that life can be as though it were over for them when the children are away! Think, if those at home longed for him in the same way that this old peasant woman had longed!

This thought made him happy, but he dared not believe in it. He had not been the sort that anybody could long for.

But what he had not been, perhaps he might become.

Round about him he saw the portraits of those who were away. They were big, strong men and women with earnest faces. There were brides in long veils, and gentlemen in fine clothes; and there were children with waved hair and pretty white dresses. And he thought that they all stared blindly into vacancy — and did not want to see.

"Poor you!" said the boy to the portraits. "Your mother is dead. You cannot make amends now for your leaving of her. But my mother is living!"

Here he paused, and nodded and smiled to himself. "My mother is living," said he. "Both father and mother are living."

CHAPTER EIGHTEEN

FROM TABERG TO HUSKVARNA

Friday, April fifteenth.

THE boy sat awake nearly all night, but toward morning he fell asleep and dreamed of his father and mother. He could hardly recognize them. They had grown gray, and had old and wrinkled faces. He asked how this had come about, and they answered that they had aged so because they had longed for him. He was both touched and astonished, for he had never believed but that they were glad to be rid of him.

When the boy awoke it was morning with fine, clear weather. First, he, himself, ate a bit of the bread which he had found in the cabin; then he gave the geese and the cow their breakfast, and opened the shed door so that the cow could go over to the nearest farm. When the neighbours saw the cow coming along all by herself they would surely understand that something was wrong with her mistress, and would hurry over to the desolate farm to see how the old woman was getting along. They would then find her dead body and bury it.

The boy and the geese had barely risen into the air, when they caught a glimpse of a high mountain, with almost perpendicular walls, and an abrupt, broken-off top; and they knew then that it was Taberg. On the summit stood Akka, with Yksi and Kaksi, Kolmi and Neljä, Viisi and Kuusi, and all six goslings — waiting for them. There was a rejoicing, and a cackling, and a fluttering, and a calling, which no one can describe, when they saw that the goosey-gander and Dunfin had succeeded in finding Thumbietot.

The woods grew rather high on Taberg's sides, but her highest peak was barren; and from there one could look far out in all directions. If one gazed toward the east, or south, or west, then there was hardly anything to be seen but a poor highland with dark spruce-trees, brown marshes, ice-clad lakes, and bluish mountain-ridges. The boy couldn't keep from thinking it was true that the one who had created this hadn't taken very great pains with his work, but had thrown it together in a hurry. But if one glanced to the north, it was altogether different. Here it looked as if it had been worked out with the greatest care and affection. In this direction one saw only beautiful mountains, soft valleys, and winding rivers, all the way to the big Lake Vettern which lay ice-free and transparently clear, and shone as if it were not filled with water but with blue light.

It was Vettern that lent such wondrous charm to the landscape north of Mount Taberg. It was as if a blue ether had risen up from the lake, and veiled the land. Groves and hills and roofs, and the spires of Jönköping City, which shimmered along Vettern's shores, lay enveloped in pale blue that caressed the eye. If there were countries in heaven, they, too, must be blue like this, thought the boy, believing that he had got a faint idea of how it must look in Paradise.

Later in the day, when the geese continued their journey, they flew up toward the blue valley. They were in holiday humour, shrieked and made such a racket that no one with ears could help hearing them.

This happened to be the first really fine spring day they had had in this section. Until now, the spring had done its work under rain and bluster; but with the sudden appearance of fine weather, the people were filled with such longing after summer warmth and green woods that they could hardly perform their tasks. And when the wild geese flew by, high above the ground, cheerful and free, all paused in their work to glance at them.

The first to sight the wild geese that day were miners on Taberg, who were digging ore at the mouth of the mine. When they heard their cackle, they paused in their drilling for ore, and one called up to the birds: "Where are you going? Where are you going?" The geese didn't understand what he said, but the boy leaned forward over the goose-back, and answered for them: "Where there is neither pick nor hammer." When the miners heard the words, they thought it was their own longing that made the goose-cackle sound like human speech. "Take us along with you! Take us along with you!" they cried. "Not this year," shrieked the boy. "Not this year."

The wild geese followed Taber River down toward Monk Lake, and all the while they made the same racket. Here, on the narrow land-strip between Monk and Vettern lakes, lay Jönköping with its great factories. First the wild geese flew over Monk Lake paper mills. The noon rest hour was just over, and the big workmen were streaming down to the mill-gate. When they heard the wild geese, they stopped a moment to listen. "Where are you going? Where are you going?" called the workmen. The wild geese understood nothing of what they said, but the boy answered for them: Where there are neither machines nor steam-boxes." When the workmen heard the answer, they believed it was their own longing that made the goose-cackle sound like human speech. "Take us along with you!" "Not this year," answered the boy. "Not this year."

Next, the geese flew over the well-known match factory, which stands on the shores of Vettern—large as a fortress—its high chimneys reaching toward the sky. Not a soul moved out in the yards; but in a large hall young working-women sat and filled match-boxes. They had opened a window, on account of the beautiful weather, and through it came the wild geese's call. The one who sat nearest the window leaned out with a match-box in her hand, and cried: "Where are you going? Where are you going?" "To that land where there is no need of either light or matches," said the boy. The girl thought that what she heard was only goose-cackle; but thinking that she had distinguished a few words, she called out in answer: "Take me along with you!" "Not this year," replied the boy. "Not this year."

East of the factories lies Jönköping, on the most glorious spot that a city can occupy. The narrow Vettern has high, steep sand-dunes, both on the eastern and on the western sides; but straight south, the sand-walls are torn down, as if to make room for a large gate, through which one reaches the lake. And in the middle of the gate—with mountains to the left, and mountains to the right; with Monk Lake behind it, and Vettern before it—lies Jönköping. The wild geese flew over the long, narrow city and behaved here just as they had done in the country. But in the city there was no one who answered them. It was not to be expected that city folk would stop in the streets, and call to wild geese.

The trip extended farther along the shores of Vettern;

and after a little they came to Sanna Sanitarium. Some of the patients were out on the veranda enjoying the spring air, and they too heard the goose-cackle. "Where are you going?" asked one in such a feeble voice that he was scarcely heard. "To that land where there is neither sorrow nor sickness," answered the boy. "Take us along with you!" said the sick ones. "Not this year," answered the boy. "Not this year."

When they had flown still farther on, they came to Huskvarna, which lay in a valley. The mountains around it were steep and beautifully formed. A river rushed along the heights in long and narrow falls. Big workshops and factories lay below the mountain walls; and scattered along the valley-bottom were the workingmen's homes, encircled by little gardens; and in the centre of the valley lay the schoolhouse. Just as the wild geese came along, a bell rang, and a crowd of school children marched out in line. They were so numerous that the whole schoolyard was soon filled with them. "Where are you going? Where are you going?" the children shouted when they heard the wild geese. "Where there are neither books nor lessons to be found," answered the boy. "Take us along!" shrieked the children. "Not this year, but next!" cried the boy. "Not this year, but next!"

Chapter Nineteen

THE BIG BIRD LAKE

JARRO, THE WILD DUCK

ON THE eastern shore of Vettern looms Mount Omberg; to the east of Omberg lies Dagmosse, and just east of Dagmosse lies Lake Tåkern. Around the whole of Tåkern spreads the wide, even Ostergota plain.

Tåkern is quite a large lake and in olden times it must have been larger still. But then the people thought it covered entirely too much of the fertile plain, so they attempted to drain the water from it, that they might sow and reap on the lake-bottom. But they did not succeed in laying waste the entire lake — which was evidently their intention — therefore it still hides a lot of land. Since the draining, the lake has become so shallow that hardly at any point is it more than a fathom deep. The shores have become marshy and muddy; and out in the lake little mud-islets stick up above the water's surface.

Now, there is one that loves to stand with feet in the water, if only the body and head are in the air, and that is the reed. And it cannot find a better place to grow upon than the long, shallow Tåkern shores, and around the little mud-islets. It thrives so well that it grows taller than a man's height, and so thick that it is almost impossible to push a boat through it It forms a broad green enclosure around the whole lake, so that it is accessible only in a few places, where the people have taken away the reeds.

But if the reeds shut the people out, they give, in return, shelter and protection to many other creatures. For in the reeds there are a lot of little dams and canals with green, still water, where duckweed and pondweed run to seed; and where gnat-eggs and blackfish and worms are hatched out in uncountable masses. And all along the shores of these little dams and canals, there are many well-secluded places where seabirds hatch their eggs, and bring up their young without being troubled by enemies or food worries.

An incredible number of birds live in the Tåkern reeds; and more and more gather there every year, as they come to know what a splendid abode it is. The first who settled there were the wild ducks, who still live there by the thousands. But they no longer own the entire lake, for they have been obliged to share it with swans, grebes, coots, loons, fen-ducks, and a lot of others.

Tåkern is certainly the largest and choicest bird lake in the whole country; and the birds may count themselves lucky so long as they own such a retreat. But it is uncertain as to how long they will be in control of reeds and mudbanks, for human beings cannot forget that the lake extends over a considerable portion of good and fertile soil; and every little while the proposition to drain it comes up among them. And if these proposals were carried out, many thousands of water-birds would be forced to move from these quarters.

At the time that Nils Holgersson travelled around with the wild geese, there lived at Tåkern a wild duck named Jarro. He was a young bird, who had only lived one summer, one fall, and a winter; now, it was his first spring. He had just returned from North Africa, having reached Tåkern in such good season that the ice was still on the lake.

One evening, while he and the other young wild ducks were having the best fun, racing back and forth over the lake, a hunter shot at them, and Jarro was wounded in the breast. He thought he would surely die; but in order that the one who had shot him shouldn't get him into his power, he continued to fly as long as he could. He didn't think whither he was directing his course, but only struggled to get far away. When his strength failed him, so that he could not fly any farther, he was no longer on the lake. He had flown a short distance inland, when he sank down, exhausted, before the entrance to one of the big farms which lie along the shores of Tåkern.

A moment later, a young farm-hand happened along. He saw Jarro, and came and lifted him up. But Jarro, who asked for nothing but to be let die in peace, gathered his waning powers and nipped the farm-hand in the finger, so he should let go of him.

Jarro could not free himself. The encounter had this good in it at any rate; the farm-hand noticed that the bird was alive. He carried him very gently into the cottage, and showed him to the mistress of the house — a young woman with a kindly face. At once she took Jarro from the farm-hand, stroked him on the back, and wiped away the blood that trickled down through the neck-feathers. She looked him over very carefully; and when she saw how pretty he was, with his dark green, shining head, his white neck-band, his brownish-red back, and his blue wing-mirror, she probably thought it would be a pity for him to die. She promptly put a basket in order, and tucked the bird into it.

All the while Jarro fluttered and struggled to get loose; but when he understood that the people had no thought of killing him, he settled down in the basket with a sense of comfort. Now it was evident how exhausted he had become from pain and loss of blood. The mistress carried the basket across the floor to place it in the corner, by the fireplace; but before she put it down Jarro was already fast asleep.

In a little while Jarro was awakened by some one nudging him gently. When he opened his eyes he experienced such an awful shock that he almost lost his senses. Now he was surely lost! for there stood *the* one who was more dangerous than either human beings or birds of prey. It was no one less than Cæsar himself! — the long-haired dog that nosed him inquisitively.

How pitifully scared had he not been the summer before, when he was still a little yellow-down duckling, every time he had heard the warning call: "Cæsar is coming! Cæsar is coming!" Whenever he had seen the brown and white spotted dog with the teeth-filled jowls come wading through the reeds, he believed that he had beheld death itself. He had always hoped that he would never have to live through that moment when he should meet Cæsar face to face.

But, to his sorrow, he must have fallen down in the very yard where Cæsar lived, for there he stood right over him. "Who are you?" he growled. "How did you get into the house? Don't you belong down among the reed banks?"

It was with great difficulty that he gained the courage to speak. "Don't be angry with me, Cæsar, because I came into the house!" he pleaded. "It isn't my fault. I have been wounded by a gunshot. It was the mistress herself who laid me in this basket."

"Oho! so it was the house-folk themselves that placed you here," said Cæsar. "Then it is surely their intention to cure you; though for my part, I think it would be more sensible for them to eat you, since you are in their power. But, at all events, you are safe in the house. You needn't look so scared. Now, we're not down on Tåkern."

With that Cæsar stretched himself full length before the blazing log-fire, to sleep. As soon as Jarro understood that this terrible danger was past, extreme lassitude crept upon him, and he fell asleep anew.

The next time Jarro awoke, he saw that a dish with grain and water stood before him. He was still quite ill, but he felt hungry nevertheless, and began to eat. When the mistress saw that he ate, she came over and petted him, and looked pleased. After that, Jarro fell asleep again. For several days he did nothing but eat and sleep.

One bright morning Jarro felt so well that he stepped from the basket and wandered along the floor. But he hadn't gone very far before he keeled over, and lay there. Then along came Cæsar, who opened his big jaws and grabbed him. Jarro believed, of course, that the dog was going to bite him to death; but Cæsar carried him back to the basket without harming him. Because of that Jarro had such confidence in the dog, Cæsar, that on his next walk in the cottage, he went over to the dog and laid down beside him. Thus Cæsar and he became good friends, and every day, for several hours, Jarro lay and slept between Cæsar's fore-paws.

But an even greater affection than he had for Cæsar, did Jarro feel toward his mistress. Of her he had not the least fear; but rubbed his head against her hand when she brought him his food. Whenever she went out from the cottage he sighed with regret; and when she came back he cried welcome to her in his own language.

Jarro forgot entirely how afraid he had been of both dogs and humans in other days. He thought now that they were gentle and kind, and he loved them. He wished that he were well, so he could fly down to Tåkern to tell the wild ducks that their enemies were not dangerous, and that they need not fear them.

He had observed that the human beings, as well as Cæsar, had calm eyes, which it did one good to look into. Clawina, the house cat, was the only one in the cottage whose glance he did not care to meet. She did him no harm either, but he couldn't place any confidence in her. Then, too, she quarrelled with him constantly, because he loved human beings. "You think they protect you because they are fond of you," said Clawina. "You just wait until you are fat enough! Then they'll wring the neck off you. I know them, I do."

Jarro, like all birds, had a tender and affectionate heart; and he was unutterably distressed when he heard this. He couldn't imagine that his mistress would wish to wring the neck off him, nor could he believe any such thing of her son, the little boy who sat for hours beside his basket, and babbled and chattered. He seemed to think that they had the same love for him that he had for them.

One day, while Jarro and Cæsar lay on their usual spot before the fire, Clawina sat on the hearth and began to tease the wild duck.

"I wonder, Jarro, what you wild ducks will do next year, when Tåkern is drained and turned into grain-fields?" said Clawina. "What's that you say, Clawina?" cried Jarro, and jumped up — scared through and through. "I always forget, Jarro, that you do not understand human speech, like Cæsar and myself," purred the cat. "Otherwise you surely would have heard the men who were here yesterday say that all the water was to be drained from Tåkern, and that next year the lake-bottom would be as dry as a house-floor. And now I wonder where you wild ducks will go." While Jarro listened to this talk he became so furious that he hissed like a snake. "You are just as mean as a common coot!" he screamed at Clawina. "You only want to incite me against human beings. I don't believe they want to do anything of the sort. They must know that Tåkern is the wild ducks' property. Why should they make so many birds homeless and unhappy? You have certainly hit upon all this to scare me. I hope that you may be torn in pieces by Gorgo, the eagle! I hope that my mistress will chop off your whiskers!"

But Jarro couldn't shut Clawina up with this outburst. "So you think I'm lying," said she. "Ask Cæsar, then! He was also in the house last night. Cæsar never lies."

"Cæsar," said Jarro, "you understand human speech much better than Clawina. Say that she hasn't heard aright! Think how it would be if the people were to drain Tåkern, and change the lake-bottom into fields! Then there would be no more pondweed or duck-food for the grown wild ducks, and no blackfish or worms or gnat-eggs for the ducklings. Then the reed-banks would disappear — where now the ducklings conceal themselves until they are able to fly. All ducks would be compelled to move away from here, and seek another home. But where shall they find a retreat like Tåkern? Cæsar, say that Clawina has not heard aright!"

It was wonderful to watch Cæsar's behaviour during this altercation. He had been wide-awake the whole time before, but now, when Jarro turned to him, he panted, laid his long nose on his fore-paws, and was sound asleep within the wink of an eyelid.

The cat looked down at Cæsar with a knowing smile. "I believe that Cæsar doesn't care to answer you," she said to Jarro. "It is with him as with all dogs; they will never admit that humans can do any wrong. But you can rely upon my word, at any rate. I shall tell you why they wish to drain the lake just now. So long as you wild ducks were still in power on Tåkern they did not wish to drain it, for then they got some good out of you; but now that grebes and coots, and other birds who are useless as food, have infested nearly all the reed-banks, the people think it needless to let the lake remain on their account."

Jarro didn't trouble himself to answer Clawina, but raised his head and shouted in Cæsar's ear: "Cæsar! You know that on Tåkern there are still so many ducks left that they fill the air like clouds. Say it isn't true that human beings intend to make all of these homeless!"

Then Cæsar sprang up with such a sudden outburst at Clawina that she had to save herself by jumping upon a shelf. "I'll teach you to keep quiet when I want to sleep," growled Cæsar. "Of course I know that there is some talk of draining the lake this year. But there has been talk of this many times before without anything coming of it. And that draining business is a matter in which I take no stock whatsoever. For how would it go with the game if Tåkern were laid waste. You're a donkey to gloat over a thing like that. What will you and I have to amuse ourselves with, when there are no more birds on Tåkern?"

THE DECOY-DUCK

Sunday, April seventeenth.

JARRO was so well now that he could fly all about the house. He was petted a good deal by the mistress, and her little boy ran out into the yard and plucked for him the first spring grass-blades. When the mistress caressed him, Jarro thought that, although he was so strong now that he could fly down to Tåkern at any time, he shouldn't care to be separated from human beings. He had no objection to remaining with them all his life.

But early one morning the mistress placed a halter, or noose, over Jarro, which prevented him from using his wings; then she turned him over to the farm-hand who had found him in the yard. The farm-hand poked him under his arm, and went down to Tåkern with him.

The ice had melted during Jarro's illness. The old, dry fall leaves still lay scattered along the shores and islets, but all the water-weeds had begun to take root down in the deep; and the green stems had already reached the surface. And now nearly all the birds of passage were at home. The curlews' hooked bills peeped out from the reeds. The grebes glided about with new feather-collars around their necks; and the jacksnipe were gathering straws for their nests.

The farm-hand got into a scow, laid Jarro in the bottom of the boat, and began to pole out. Jarro, who had now accustomed himself to expect only good of human beings, said to Cæsar, who was also of the party, that he felt very grateful toward the farm-hand for taking him out on the lake. But the man needn't keep him so tightly fettered for he was not thinking of flying away. To this

Cæsar made no reply. He was very close-mouthed that morning.

The only thing which struck Jarro as being a bit strange was that the farm-hand had taken his gun along. He couldn't believe that any of the good folk in the cottage would want to shoot at birds. And, besides, Cæsar had told him that the people didn't hunt at this time of the year. "It is a prohibited time," he had said, "although this doesn't concern me, of course."

The farm-hand rowed over to one of the little reed-enclosed mud-islets. There he stepped from the boat, gathered some old reeds into a pile, and laid down behind it. Jarro was free to wander around on the ground with the halter over his wings, and tethered to the boat with a long string.

Suddenly Jarro caught sight of some young ducks and drakes, in whose company he had formerly raced back and forth over the lake. They were a long way off, but Jarro called them to him with loud shouts. They responded, and a large and beautiful flock approached. Even before they were there, Jarro began to tell them about his marvellous rescue, and of the kindness of human beings. Just then, bang went two shots behind him, and three ducks sank down in the reeds — lifeless. Cæsar bounded out and captured them.

Then Jarro understood. The human beings had saved him only that they might use him as a decoy-duck. And they had also succeeded. Three ducks had been killed on his account. He thought he should die of shame. He fancied that even his friend Cæsar looked contemptuously at him; and when they got back to the cottage, he didn't dare lie down and sleep beside the dog.

The next morning Jarro was again taken out to the

shallows. This time, also, he sighted some ducks. But when he observed that they flew toward him, he called to them: "Away! Away! Be careful! Fly in another direction! There's a hunter hidden behind the reed-pile. I'm only a decoy-bird!" And he actually succeeded in preventing their coming within shooting distance.

Jarro hardly had time to taste of a grass-blade, so busy was he keeping watch. He called out his warning as soon as a bird drew nigh. He even warned the grebes, although he detested them because they crowded the ducks out of their best hiding-places. But he did not wish that any bird should meet with misfortune on his account. And, thanks to Jarro's vigilance, the farm-hand had to go home without firing a single shot.

All the same, Cæsar looked less displeased than on the previous day; and when the evening was come he took Jarro in his mouth, carried him over to the fireplace, and let him sleep between his fore-paws.

Nevertheless, Jarro was no longer contented in the cottage, but was grievously unhappy. His heart suffered at the thought that humans never had loved him. When the mistress or the little boy came forward to caress him, he stuck his bill under his wing and pretended that he slept.

For several days Jarro continued his distressful watch-service; and he was already known over the whole lake. Then it happened one morning, while he called out as usual: "Have a care, birds! Don't come near me! I'm only a decoy-duck," that a grebe-nest came floating toward the shallows where he was tied. There was nothing extraordinary about this. It was a nest from the year before; and since grebe-nests are built in such a way that they can move on water like boats, it often happens that they drift out on the lake. Yet Jarro stood there gazing toward nest, which was headed so straight for the islet that it appeared as if some one were steering its course over the water.

As the nest came nearer, Jarro saw that a little human being — the tiniest he had ever seen — sat in the nest and rowed forward with a pair of sticks. And this little human called to him: "Go as near the water as you can, Jarro, and be ready to fly. You shall soon be freed."

A few seconds later the grebe-nest lay near land, yet the little oarsman did not leave it, but sat huddled between branches and straw. Jarro, too, held himself almost rigid. He was actually paralyzed with fear lest the rescuer should be discovered.

And next a flock of wild geese came flying over. Then Jarro woke up to business, and warned them with loud shrieks; but in spite of this they flew back and forth over the shallows several times. They held themselves so high that they were beyond shooting distance; still the farm-hand let himself be tempted to shoot at them. These shots were hardly fired when the little creature ran up on land, drew a tiny knife from its sheath, and, with two quick strokes, cut loose Jarro's halter. "Now fly away, Jarro, before the man has time to load again!" cried he, while he himself ran down to the grebe-nest and poled away from the shore.

The hunter's gaze was fixed upon the geese, and he hadn't noticed that Jarro had been freed; but Cæsar knew what had happened; and just as Jarro lifted his wings, he dashed forward and grabbed him by the neck.

Jarro cried pitifully; and the boy who had freed him said quietly to Cæsar: "If you are just as honourable as you look, surely you cannot wish to force a good bird to sit here and entice others into trouble."

When Cæsar heard these words, he grinned viciously with his upper lip, but the next second he dropped Jarro. "Fly, Jarro!" said he. "You are certainly too good to be a decoy-duck. It wasn't for this that I wanted to keep you here; but because it will be lonely in the cottage without you.

THE LOWERING OF THE LAKE

Wednesday, April twentieth.

IT WAS indeed very lonely in the cottage without Jarro. The dog and the cat found the time long, when they didn't have him to wrangle over; and the housewife missed the glad quacking with which he had welcomed her every time she entered the house. But the one who longed most for Jarro was the little boy, Per Ola. He was but three years old, and the only child; and in all his life he had never had a playmate like Jarro. When he heard that Jarro had gone back to Tåkern and the wild ducks, he couldn't be reconciled to this, but thought constantly of how he should get him back again.

Per Ola had talked a good deal with Jarro, while he lay in his basket, and he was certain that the duck had understood him. He begged his mother to take him down to the lake that he might find Jarro, and persuade him to come back to them. Mother wouldn't listen to this; but the little one didn't give up his plan for all that.

The day after Jarro had disappeared, Per Ola was running about in the yard. He played by himself, as usual, while Cæsar lay on the stoop; and when mother let the boy out, she said: "Take good care of Per Ola, Cæsar!"

Now if all had been as usual, Cæsar would have obeyed the command, and the boy would have been so well guarded that he couldn't have run the least risk. But Cæsar was not himself these days. He knew that the farmers who lived around Tåkern had held frequent conferences about the lowering of the lake; and that the matter was almost settled. The ducks must leave and Cæsar would nevermore behold a glorious chase. He was so preoccupied with the thought of this misfortune, that he did not remember to watch over Per Ola.

The little one had scarcely been alone in the yard a minute, before he realized that now the right moment was come to go down to Tåkern and talk with Jarro. He opened the gate, and wandered down toward the lake on the narrow path which ran along the banks. As long as he could be seen from the house, he walked slowly; but afterward he quickened his stride. He was very much afraid that mother, or some one else, should call out to him that he couldn't go. He didn't wish to do anything naughty, only to persuade Jarro to come home; but he felt that the folks at home would not have approved of the undertaking.

When Per Ola came down to the shore, he called Jarro many times. Thereupon he stood a long while and waited, but no Jarro appeared. He saw several birds that resembled the wild duck, but they flew by without noticing him, and he could understand that none among them was the right one.

When Jarro didn't come to him, the little boy thought that it would be easier to find him were he to go out on the lake. There were several good craft lying along the shore, but these were tied. The one that lay loose, and at liberty, was an old leaky scow which was so unfit that no one thought of using it. But Per Ola scrambled into it not caring that the whole bottom was filled with water. He had not strength enough to use the oars, but, instead, sat down and began to rock the scow. Certainly no grown person would have succeeded in moving a boat out on Tåkern in that manner; but when the tide is high and ill-luck to the fore, little children have a marvellous faculty for getting out to sea. Per Ola was soon drifting around on Tåkern, calling for Jarro.

While the old scow was being rocked like this, out to sea, the cracks opened wider and wider, and the water actually streamed into it. Per Ola didn't pay the slightest attention to this. He sat upon the little bench in front and called to every bird he saw, and wondered why Jarro didn't appear.

At last Jarro caught sight of Per Ola. He heard that some one called him by the name which he had borne among human beings, and he understood that the boy had gone out on Tåkern to search for him. Jarro was unspeakably happy to find that one of the humans really loved him. He shot down toward Per Ola like an arrow, seated himself beside him, and let him caress him. They were very happy to see each other again. But suddenly Jarro noticed the condition of the scow. It was half filled with water, and almost ready to sink. Jarro tried to tell Per Ola that he, who could neither fly nor swim, must try to get upon land; but Per Ola didn't understand him. Then Jarro did not wait an instant, but hurried away to get help.

In a little while he returned, carrying on his back a tiny creature who was much smaller than Per Ola himself. Had he not been able to talk and move, the boy would have believed that it was a doll. Instantly, the little one ordered Per Ola to pick up a long, slender pole that lay in the bottom of the scow, and try to paddle toward one of the reed-islands. Per Ola obeyed him, and he and the tiny creature together steered the scow. With a couple of strokes they were over by little reed-encircled island, and now Per Ola was told that he must step ashore. And just the very moment that Per Ola set foot on land, the scow filled up with water and sank to the bottom.

When Per Ola saw this he was sure that his father and mother would be very angry with him. He would have started in to cry if he hadn't just then found something else to think of: A flock of big, gray birds suddenly lighted on the island. The little midget took him over to them, and told him their names, and what they said. And this was so funny that Per Ola forgot everything else.

Meanwhile the folks on the farm had discovered that the boy was missing, and were searching for him. They searched the outhouses, looked in the well, and hunted through the cellar. Then they went out into highways and by-paths; wandered to the neighbouring farm to find out if he had strayed over there, and they searched for him also down by Tåkern. But no matter where they sought they did not find him.

The dog Cæsar understood very well that the farmer-folk were looking for Per Ola, but he did nothing to put them on the right track; instead he lay still, as if the matter didn't concern him.

Later in the day, Per Ola's footprints were discovered down by the boat-landing. Then they found that the old, leaky scow was no longer on the strand. And now they began to understand how it had all come about.

The farmer and his helpers immediately took out the boats and went in search of the boy. They rowed around on Tåkern until late in the evening, without seeing the least shadow of him. They couldn't help believing that the old scow had gone down, and that the little one lay dead at the bottom of the lake.

All the evening, Per Ola's mother hunted round on the strand. Every one else was convinced that the boy was drowned, but she could not bring herself to believe that. She searched all the while. She searched between reeds and bullrushes; tramped and tramped on the muddy shore, never thinking of how deep her foot sank, or how wet she had become. She was unspeakably desperate. Her heart ached in her breast. She did not weep, but wrung her hands and called for her child in loud piercing tones.

Round about her she heard swans' and ducks' and curlews' shrieks. She thought that they followed her, and moaned and wailed — they too. "Surely, they, too, must be in trouble, since they moan so." Then she remembered: these were only birds that she heard complain. They surely had no worries.

It was strange that they did not quiet down after sunset. She heard all these uncountable bird-throngs which lived along Tåkern send forth cry upon cry. Several of them followed her wherever she went; others came rustling past on light wings. All the air was filled with moans and lamentations.

But the anguish which she herself was suffering opened her heart. She felt that she was not so far removed from all other living creatures as people usually think. She understood better than ever before, how birds fared. They had their constant worries for home and children, they, as she. There was certainly not such a great difference between them and her as she had heretofore believed.

Then she happened to think that it was as good as settled

that these thousands of swans and ducks and loons would lose their homes here by Tåkern. "It will be very hard for them," she thought. "Where shall they bring up their children now?"

She paused and pondered: It appeared to be an excellent and agreeable accomplishment to change a lake into fields and meadows, but let it be some other lake than Tåkern; some other lake, which was not the home of so many thousand creatures.

She remembered how on the following day the proposition to lower the lake was to be decided, and she wondered if this was why her little son had been lost — just to-day.

Was it God's meaning that sorrow should come to open her heart — just to-day — before it was too late to avert the cruel act?

She walked rapidly up to the house, and began to talk with her husband about this. She spoke of the lake, and of the birds, and said that she believed it was God's judgment on them both. She soon found that he was of the same opinion.

They already owned a large place, but if the lake-draining were carried into effect, such a goodly portion of the lake-bottom would fall to their share that their property would be nearly doubled. For this reason they had been more eager for the undertaking than any of the other shore owners. The others had been worried about expenses, and anxious lest the draining should not prove any more successful this time than it was the last. Per Ola's father knew in his heart that it was he who had influenced them to undertake the work. He had exercised all his eloquence, so that he might leave to his son a farm as large again as his father had left to him.

He stood and wondered if God's hand was back of the fact that Tåkern had taken his son from him on the day before he was to have drawn up the contract to lay it waste. The wife didn't have to say many words to him, before he answered: "It may be that God does not want us to interfere with His order. I'll talk with the others about this to-morrow, and I think we'll decide that all may remain as it is."

While the farmer-folk were talking this over, Cæsar lay before the fire. He raised his head and listened very attentively. When he thought that he was sure of the outcome, he walked up to the mistress, took her by the skirt, and led her to the door. "But Cæsar!" said she, trying to break away from him, "do you know where Per Ola is?" she cried out. Cæsar barked joyfully, and threw himself against the door. She opened it, and the dog dashed down toward Tåkern. The mistress was so positive that he knew where Per Ola was that she rushed after him. And no sooner had they reached the shore than they heard a child's cry out on the lake.

Per Ola had had the best day of his life, in company with Thumbietot and the birds; but now he had begun to cry because he was hungry and afraid of the darkness. And he was glad when father and mother and Cæsar came for him.

Chapter Twenty

ULVÅSA-LADY

THE PROPHECY

Friday, April twenty-second.

ONE night, when the boy lay sleeping on an island in Tåkern, he was awakened by oar-strokes. He had hardly got his eyes open when there fell such a dazzling light on them that it made him blink.

At first he couldn't make out what it was that shone so brightly out here on the lake; but soon he saw that a scow, with a big burning torch set up on a spike, aft, lay near the edge of the reeds. The red flame from the torch was clearly reflected in the night-dark lake; and the brilliant light must have tempted the fish, for in the water were seen a mass of dark specks that moved continually, and changed places.

There were two old men in the scow. One sat at the oars, the other stood on a bench in the stern and held in his hand a short spear, which was coarsely barbed. The one who rowed was apparently a poor fisherman. He was small, dried-up, and weather-beaten, and wore a thin, threadbare coat. It was plain that he was so used to being out in all sorts of weather that he didn't mind the cold. The other was well fed and well dressed, and looked like a prosperous and self-complacent farmer.

"Stop now!" said the farmer, when they were opposite the island where the boy lay. At the same time he plunged the spear into the water. When he drew it out again a long, fine eel came with it.

"Look at that!" he said as he released the eel from the spear. "That wasn't a bad catch, eh? Now we have so many that I think we can turn back."

His comrade did not lift the oars, but sat looking around. "It is lovely out here on the lake to-night," he said. And so it was. The water was perfectly calm, so that its entire surface lay in undisturbed rest, save the narrow strips where the boat had gone forward. This lay like a path of gold. and glittered in the firelight. The sky was a clear deep blue, and thickly studded with stars. The shores were hidden by the reed islands except toward the west, where Mount Omberg loomed high and dark, cutting away a big, three-cornered piece of the domelike sky.

The farmer turned his head to get the light out of his eyes, then looked about him. "Yes, it is lovely here in Östergylln," said he. "Still the best thing about the province is not its beauty." "Then what is it that's best?" asked the oarsman. "That it has always been a respected and honoured province." "That may be true enough." "And then this, that one knows it will always continue to be so." "But how in the world can one know that?" said the one who sat at the oars.

The farmer straightened up where he stood and braced himself with the spear. "There is an old legend which has been handed down from father to son in my family; and in it one learns what will happen to Ostergötland." "Then you may as well tell it to me," said the oarsman. "We do not tell it to any one and every one, but I don't wish to keep it a secret from an old comrade.

"At Ulvåsa, here in Ostergötland," he continued (and

one could tell by the tone of his voice that he talked of something which he had heard from others, and knew by heart), "many, many years ago, there lived a lady who had the gift of looking into the future, and telling people what was going to happen to them — just as certainly and accurately as though it had already occurred. For this she became widely noted; and it is easy to understand why people from both far and near came to her, to find out what they were to pass through of good or evil.

"One day, when Ulvåsa-lady sat in her hall and spun, as was the custom in former days, a poor peasant came into the room and seated himself on the bench near the door.

"'I wonder what you are sitting and thinking about, dear lady,' said the peasant after a little.

"'I am sitting and thinking about high and holy things,' she answered. 'Then it is not fitting, perhaps, that I ask you about something which weighs on my heart,' said the peasant.

"'It is probably nothing else that weighs on your heart than that you may reap much grain on your field. But I am accustomed to receive communications from the Emperor, as to how it will go with his crown; and from the Pope, as to how it will go with his keys.' 'Such things cannot be easy to answer,' said the peasant. 'I have heard also that no one goes from here without being dissatisfied with what he has heard.'

"When the peasant said that, he noticed that Ulvåsa-lady bit her lip, and moved farther up on the bench. 'So this is what you have heard of me,' she said. 'Then you may as well tempt fortune by asking me about the thing you wish to know; and you shall see whether or not I can answer so that you will be satisfied.'

"After this the peasant did not hesitate to state his errand. He said that he had come to ask how it would go with Östergötland in the future. There was nothing which was so dear to him as his native province, and he felt that he would be happy until his dying day if he could get a satisfactory reply to his query.

"'Oh!' if that is all you wish to know,' said the wise lady; 'then I think that you will be content. For here, where I now sit, I can tell you that it will be like this with Östergötland: it will always have something to boast of ahead of other provinces.'

"'Yes, that was a good answer, dear lady,' said the peasant,' and I should now be entirely at peace if I only knew how such a thing could be possible.'

"'Why should it not be possible?' said Ulvåsa-lady. 'Don't you know that Östergötland is already renowned? Or think you there is any place in Sweden that can boast of possessing, at the same time, two such cloisters as the ones in Alvastra and Vreta, and such a beautiful cathedral as the one at Linköping?'

"'That may be so,' said the peasant. 'But I'm an old man, and I know that people's minds are changeable. I fear that there will come a time when they won't give us any glory, for either Alvastra or Vreta, or even for the cathedral.'

"'Herein you may be right,' said Ulvåsa-lady, 'but you need not doubt prophecy on that account. I shall now build up a new cloister on Vadstena, and this will become the most celebrated in the North. Thither both the high and the lowly shall make pilgrimages, and all shall sing the praises of the province because it has so holy a place within its confines.'

"The peasant replied that he was right glad to know this. But he also knew, of course, that everything was perishable; and he wondered much what would give distinction to the province, if Vadstena Cloister should once fall into disrepute.

"'You are not easy to satisfy,' said Ulvåsa-lady, 'but surely I can see far enough ahead to tell you that before Vadstena Cloister shall have lost its splendour there will be a castle erected close by, which will be the most magnificent of its period. Kings and dukes will be guests there, and it shall be accounted an honour to the whole province that it owns such an ornament.''

"'This I am also glad to hear,' said the peasant. 'But I'm an old man, and I know how it generally turns out with this world's glories. And if the castle goes to ruin, I wonder much what there will be that can attract the people's attention to this province?'

"'It's not a little that you want to know,' said Ulvåsa-lady, 'but, certainly, I can look far enough into the future to see that there will be life and movement in the forests around Finspång. I see how cabins and smithies arise there, and I believe that the whole province shall become renowned because iron will be moulded within its confines.'

"The peasant didn't deny that he was delighted to hear this. 'But if it should go so badly that even Finspång's foundry went down in importance, then it would hardly be possible that any new thing could arise of which Östergötland might boast.'

"'You are not easy to please,' said Ulvåsa-lady, 'but I can see so far into the future that I mark how, along the lake shores, great manors, large as castles, are built by gentlemen who have carried on wars in foreign lands. I believe that the manors will bring the province just as much honour as anything else that I have named.'

"'But if there comes a time when no one lauds the great manors?' insisted the peasant.

"'You need not be uneasy at all events,' said Ulvåsa-lady. 'I see how health-springs bubble on Medevi meadows, by Vättern's shores. I believe that the wells at Medevi will bring the land as much praise as you can desire.'

"'That is a mighty good thing to know,' said the peasant. 'But if there comes a time when people seek their health at other springs?'

"'You must not give yourself any anxiety on that account,' answered Ulvåsa-lady. 'I see how people dig and labour, from Motala to Mem. They dig a canal right through the country, and Östergötland's praise is again on every one's lips.'

"But, nevertheless, the peasant looked distraught.

"'I see that the rapids in Motala stream begin to draw wheels,' said Ulvåsa-lady — and now two bright red spots came to her cheeks, for she began to be impatient — 'I hear hammers resound in Motala, and looms clatter in Norrköping.'

"'Yes, that's good to know,' said the peasant, 'but everything is perishable, and I'm afraid that even this can be forgotten, and go into oblivion.'

"When the peasant was not satisfied even now, there was an end to the lady's patience. 'You say that everything is perishable,' said she, 'but now I shall name something which will always be like itself; and that is that such arrogant and pig-headed peasants as you will always be found in this province — until the end of time.'

"Hardly had Ulvåsa-lady finished speaking before the

peasant rose — happy and gratified — and thanked her for a good answer. Now, at last, he was satisfied, he said.

"Then said Ulvåsa-lady: 'Verily, I understand now how you look at it.'

"'Well, I look at it in this way, dear lady,' spoke the peasant, 'that everything which kings and priests and noblemen and merchants build and accomplish can endure only for a few years. But when you tell me that in Östergötland there will always be peasants who are honour-loving and persevering, then I know also that it will be able to preserve its ancient glory. For it is only those who go bent under the eternal labour with the soil, who can hold this land in good repute and honour — from one time to another.'"

Chapter Twenty-One

THE HOMESPUN CLOTH

Saturday, April twenty-third.

THE boy rode forward — away up in the air. He had the great Östergötland plain under him, and he sat and counted the many white churches which towered above the small leafy groves around them. It wasn't long until he had counted fifty. After that he became confused and lost track of the counting.

Nearly all the farms were built up with large, white-painted two-story houses, which looked so imposing that the boy couldn't help admiring them. "There can't be any peasants in this land," he said to himself, "since I do not see any farms."

Immediately all the wild geese shrieked: "Here the peasants live like gentlemen! Here the peasants live like gentlemen!"

On the plains the ice and snow had disappeared and the spring work had been started. "What kind of long crabs are those crawling over the fields?" asked the boy. "Ploughs and oxen. Ploughs and oxen," answered the wild geese.

The oxen moved so slowly down on the fields, that one could scarcely perceive they were in motion, and the geese shouted to them: "You won't get there before next year! You won't get there before next year!" But the oxen were equal to the occasion. They raised their muzzles in the air and bellowed: "We do more good in an hour than such as you do in a whole lifetime."

In a few places the ploughs were drawn by horses. They went along with much more eagerness and haste than the oxen; but the geese couldn't keep from teasing these either. "Aren't you ashamed to be doing ox-duty?" they cried. "Aren't you ashamed yourselves to be doing lazy man's duty?" the horses neighed back at them.

But while horses and oxen were at work in the fields, the stable ram walked about in the barnyard. He was newly clipped and irritable; he knocked over the small boys, chased the shepherd dog into his kennel, and then strutted about as though he alone were lord of the whole place. "Rammie, Rammie, what have you done with your wool?" asked the wild geese, who rode by up in the air. "That I have sent to Drag's woollen mills in Norrköping," replied the ram with a long, drawnout bleat. "Rammie, Rammie, what have you done with your horns?" asked the geese. But any horns the rammie had never possessed, to his sorrow, and one couldn't offer him a greater insult than to ask after them. He ran around a long time, and butted at the air, so furious was he.

Along the country road came a man driving a herd of Skåne pigs that were not more than a few weeks old, and were to be sold up country. They trotted along bravely, little as they were, and kept close together — as if seeking protection. "Nuff, nuff, nuff, we came away too soon from father and mother. Nuff, nuff, nuff, what is to become of us poor children," squealed the little pigs. The wild geese didn't have the heart to tease such poor little creatures. "It will be better for you than you can ever believe," they cried encouragingly, as they flew past them.

"DOWN IN THE ROAD STOOD OSA, THE GOOSE-GIRL, AND HER BROTHER, LITTLE MATS, LOOKING AT A TINY WOODEN SHOE"

The wild geese were never so merry as when flying over a flat country. Then they did not hurry themselves, but flew from farm to farm, and joked with the tame animals.

As the boy rode over the plain he happened to think of a legend which he had heard a long time ago. He didn't remember it exactly, but it was something about a petticoat, half of which was made of gold-woven velvet, and half of gray homespun. But the one who owned the petticoat had decorated the homespun with such heaps of pearls and precious stones that it looked richer and more gorgeous than the gold-cloth.

He remembered this about the homespun as he looked down on Östergötland, because it was made up of a large plain, which lay wedged in between two mountainous forest-tracts — one to the north, the other to the south. The two forest-heights lay there, a lovely blue, and shimmered in the morning light, as if bedecked with golden veils; and the plain, which spread out one winter-naked field after another, was in and of itself more beautiful than the gray homespun.

But the people must have been contented on the plain, because it was generous and kind, and they had tried to decorate it in the best possible way. High up — where the boy rode by — he thought that cities and farms, churches and factories, castles and railway stations were scattered over it, like large and small trinkets. The roofs and the window-panes glittered like jewels. Yellow country roads, shining railway-tracks and blue canals ran along between the districts, like embroidered loops. Linköping lay around its cathedral like a pearl-setting around a precious stone; and the gardens in the country were like little brooches and buttons. There was not much regulation in the pattern, but it was a display of grandeur of which one might never tire.

The geese had left Öberg and were travelling eastward along Göta Canal. This was also making itself ready for the summer. Workmen were building canal-banks, and tarring the huge lock-gates. They were working everywhere to receive spring fittingly, even in the cities. There, masons and painters stood on scaffoldings and made fine the exteriors of the houses while maids cleaned the windows. Down at the harbour, sailboats and steamers were being washed and dressed up.

At Norrköping the wild geese left the plain, and flew up toward Kolmården. For a time they had been following an old and hilly country road, which wound around cliffs and ran forward under wild mountain-walls — when the boy suddenly let out a shriek. He had been sitting and swinging his foot back and forth, and one of his wooden shoes had slipped off.

"Goosey-gander, goosey-gander, I have dropped my shoe!" cried the boy. The goosey-gander turned about and sank toward the ground; then the boy saw two children walking along the road, one of whom had picked up his shoe. "Goosey-gander, goosey-gander," screamed the boy excitedly, "fly upward again! It is too late. I can't get my shoe back now."

Down on the road stood Osa, the goose-girl, and her brother, little Mats, looking at a tiny wooden shoe that had fallen from the skies.

Osa, the goose-girl, stood silent a long while — puzzled over the find. At last she said, slowly and thoughtfully: "Do you remember, little Mats, that when we went past Övid Cloister we heard that the folks in a farmyard had seen an elf who was dressed in leather breeches, and had wooden shoes on his feet, like any other workingman? And do you recollect that when we came to Vittskövle a girl told us that she had seen a Goa-Nisse, with wooden shoes, who flew away on the back of a goose? And when we ourselves came home to our cabin, little Mats, we saw a goblin who was dressed in the same way, and who also straddled the back of a goose — and flew away. Maybe it was the same one who rode along on his goose up here in the air and dropped his wooden shoe."

"Yes, it must have been," said little Mats.

They turned the wooden shoe about and examined it carefully — for it isn't every day that one happens across Goa-Nisse's wooden shoe on the highway.

"Wait, wait, little Mats!" said Osa, the goose-girl, "There is something written on one side of it."

"Why, so there is! but they are such tiny letters."

"Let me see! It says — it says: 'Nils Holgersson from W. Vemmenhög.' That's the most wonderful thing I've ever heard!" said little Mats.

[Concluded in "*Further Adventures of Nils.*"]

GLOSSARY

TABLE OF PRONUNCIATION

The final *e* is sounded in Skåne, Sirle, Gripe, etc.

The å in Skåne and Småland is pronounced like *o* in ore.

j is like the English *y*. Nuolja, Oviksfjällen, Sjangeli, Jarro, etc., should sound as if they were spelled like this: Nuolya, Oviksfyellen, Shang-e-lee, Yarro, etc.

g, when followed by *e, i, y, ä, ö*, is also like *y*. Example Göta is pronounced Yöta.

When *g* is followed by *a, o, u*, or *å*, it is hard, as in go.

k in Norrköping, Linköping, Kivik (pronounced Chee-veek), etc., is like *ch* in cheer.

k is hard when it precedes *a, o, u*, or *å*. Example, Kaksi, Kolmi, etc.

ä is pronounced like *ā* in fare. Example, Färs.

There is no sound in the English language which corresponds to the Swedish *ö*. It is like the French *eu* in jeu.

Gripe is pronounced Greep-e.

In Sirle, the first syllable has the same sound as the *sir* in sirup.

The names which Miss Lagerlöf has given to the animals are descriptive.

Smirre Fox, is cunning fox.

Sirle Squirrel, is graceful, or nimble squirrel.

Gripe Otter, means grabbing or clutching otter.

Mårten gåskarl (Morten Goosey-gander) is a pet name for a tame gander, just as we use Dickie-bird for a pet bird.

Fru is the Swedish for Mrs. This title is usually applied to gentlewomen only. The author has used this meaning of "fru."

A Goa-Nisse is an elf-king, and corresponds to the English Puck or Robin Goodfellow.

TRANSLATOR.